Dear Arnie,

Thank you for being a wonderful partner and best friend!

SUSAN BECK KORMAN

Tales from the Old Oak Table

A Family Memoir

Thanks too for making my life journey a happy one. Your love, patience & encouragement are much appreciated.

This labor of love couldn't have been completed without you.

Love Always,
Sue

Copyright © 2012 Publisher Name
All rights reserved.

ISBN: 1479261815
ISBN 13:9781479261819
Library of Congress Control Number: 2012916670
CreateSpace Independent Publishing Platform
North Charleston, South Carolina

DEDICATION

This book is dedicated to Ned, Neil, Julie, Brad, Ross and Lynn, their children, and all future descendants

TABLE OF CONTENTS

Part I – **Beginnings**

1	Prophecy in Face of Fear	3
2	Unlikely Farmers	5
3	Digging into Our Roots	9
4	Mama's Origins	12
5	Their American Dream	17
6	Quaker Street, the Village	19
7	Living Vicariously on the Farm	21
8	Urban Homestead	23
9	Window on the World	25
10	My Big Bang	29
11	Tiny Tiger Triggers Epic Turn	33

Part II – **Daly Avenue, The Bronx – Circa 1940s and 1950s**

12	New Residents Revive Old Residence	39
13	Welcoming Committee of One	42
14	Humble Estate	45
15	Streetscape	47
16	Living Standards Rise as Enemies Fall	49
17	Shangri-La in the City	50
18	Next Door Neighbors	52
19	Coming to My Senses	54
20	Rhode Island Reds Roost Here	56
21	Characters Welcome	59

Part III — Profiles of Primary Players

22	Dad	65
23	Mama	69
24	Big Brother	76
25	Big Sister	79
26	Baby Sister	84
27	Pets are Players Too	87

Part IV — Family Matters — Circa 1940's and 1950's

28	Tales of the Round Oak Table	95
29	Kindergarten Dropout	97
30	Room to Let	100
31	Provisions for Cold Winters	105
32	Daddy's Little Helper	107
33	Here Comes Santa — Not	110
34	Goodbye to Teacher Who Turned the Tide	112
35	Coming of Age in the Fifties	114
36	Dropout Returns to School of Discontent	116
37	The Prodigal Daughter Returns	119
38	Music to Mama's Ears Only	122
39	Good Old Teddy Roosevelt High School	124
40	Pondering Pop's Pompoms	127
41	All Gangs Are Not Created Equal	130
42	Korean Conflict Hits Home	134
43	Cold Introduction to World of Commerce	138
44	Ripley's Believe It or Not	140
45	Anatomy of a Career — Setting the Course	143
46	Ticket to Ride	146
47	Dad's Cutting Triple Play	149
48	Full Charge Ahead	152
49	Career Proceeds as Advertised	155

Part V — 1960s Turning Points

50	Decade of Change-Defining Moments	161
51	Beginning of the End	166
52	Dad Loses Heart	169
53	The Horror of Halloween 1964	173
54	Road Bump Jolts Career	175
55	Generation III-All Americans	179
56	Two Women Alone in Urban Wasteland	181
57	Bronx Tale Closing Moments	184
58	End of an Era	187

Part VI — Eastward Bound

59	Crossing the Bridge	191
60	Gold Coast Calls	193
61	Crowning a Career	196
62	Better Times Prove Fleeting	198
63	Mom Faces Life's Final Challenge	200

Part VII — Moving Forward

64	Lifelong Friendship to Partners for Life	207
65	Marrying a Family	210
66	New House Stirs Old and New-found Memories	214
67	Family Reunions, Best and Worst	217
68	Car Careens into Arnie, Impacts My Career	219
69	Search for Meaningful Encore	224
70	Keeping Family Alive	231

This book is based on personal encounters, stories told to me by my parents, older siblings, aunts and other relatives. No attempt has been made to dig into genealogic sources. While many have become available since the advent of the internet, they would not work in our case. The reasons will become apparent as you read about our ancestors' native lands, name changes and circuitous journeys.

No names have been changed to preserve memories of the true characters. The incidents are true to the best of my recollection and that of those who told me about them. Events have been compressed and reordered to attempt some degree of continuity of the narrative. All dialogue is as close as possible to actual conversation as I remember it.

PREFACE

For most of my life, I felt isolated, left out, different. I thought, if only I knew more about my family; like so many others, I yearned for a human connection to my origins – a feeling of belonging, of understanding where I came from – of why I am who I am.

Revolutionary and promising as they are, the latest DNA technology, social networking and ancestral web sites cannot help us get to know our families close-up and personal.

That is why, for the last ten years, I have been writing memoir essays to introduce my nuclear family to future generations; to give them a rare opportunity to get to know their ancestors as I did. And, to help provide that oft sought after link to their beginnings.

In the course of reading these pieces aloud at writing workshops, lots of people – regardless of age, ethnic background or culture – identified with them. Older listeners summoned reminiscences of growing up during and immediately after World War II and reflected on how much society has changed. Younger ones enjoyed being introduced to a different time – before technology took over our lives – when community, close-knit families and neighborhoods played a pivotal role in shaping us.

The heart of this collection takes place in and around our home in the Bronx from the mid-forties to nineteen seventy, a telling time of economic, cultural and technological change throughout society. It begins with a brief history at the turn of the last century and ends with events that followed our farewell to a devastated neighborhood that was once a nourishing environment for the working middle class, and it takes us to the turn to the twenty-first century.

I realize many gaps still exist and regret that I did not have the foresight to ask more questions while I had the opportunity. Still, knowing the uncertainties of this life and how toward the end of the day memories tend to diminish, I believe it is time to pass on our heritage as best as I know it.

My good fortune to have lived beyond the biblical "three-score and ten," plus the distinction of being the oldest living member of this family, offer me a unique perspective and put me in the time-honored position of "custodian of the family legacy."

As such, it is my desire to offer a little insight into our roots, a glimpse of what our ancestors were really like, the times in which they lived, the challenges they overcame. I hope that, in some small way, this work will help connect present and future generations to those who came before and to help enrich life's journey.

Part I
Beginnings

Chapter I
Prophecy in Face of Fear

"The baby is coming, the baby is coming" Mama shouted her eyes wide with fear. "Where is the doctor? How can he get here in the snow," she pressed for answers.

A particularly blustery blizzard had dropped eighteen inches of snow. Dr. Walker was on his way, feverishly trying to navigate slippery country roads; blowing snow created severe whiteout conditions with visibility near zero.

"What will we do now?" Mama sobbed between increasingly rapid contractions. "We can't take care of two children, how are we going to manage with three?"

Alice, The midwife, who had battled her way through the storm earlier, stroked Mama's head, smiled and proclaimed:

"Don't worry Helen. This baby will give you lots of pleasure and will be there for you in times of need. You will be happy she came into your life. Mark my words."

Mama was grateful for the kind words; given recent events, however, she couldn't help but think: *the last thing we need right now is another baby — another mouth to feed.*

The doctor arrived minutes before my grand entrance shortly after 7:00am. I was swollen, crying and crimson with a body temperature of 104 degrees. The young country physician had never encountered this set of symptoms. When, after several hours, I still hadn't passed water and my fever remained high he anxiously announced:

"We have to take her to the hospital! They may have to do exploratory surgery."

"It's too far away," Mama whimpered. "I don't want her to have surgery."

"I can't tell what's going on here; she may not have kidneys for all we know!"

Daddy understood the doctor's concerns and at the same time shared Mama's fears about taking a newborn forty miles away to a hospital in Albany in a snowstorm, let alone having to possibly perform surgery on her tiny body.

"Let's just wait until morning. I'll watch her carefully through the night and if she stays the same you can take her to the hospital tomorrow," Daddy pleaded.

"I don't know," the doctor replied, "she could die by then."

After a short deliberation, however, he reluctantly decided to go along with the plan and left for home for some much needed rest.

After several more hours passed with no improvement, Daddy tried an old world remedy that healed almost any ailment. He placed several irons on the coal stove. When they were hot he wrapped them in towels and cautiously positioned them around my small distended body. Within a half-hour it worked; my bladder emptied. Soon the redness began to fade, the puffiness slowly receded, and I became cool to the touch.

When Doctor Walker arrived the next morning, ready to cart me off to the hospital Daddy greeted him at the door.

"She's OK. She urinated and her fever is down," he exclaimed.

The doctor was elated to find that I did, indeed, have working kidneys that were likely infected. He examined me and left behind a drug to take care of the infection, possibly Penicillin, the magic cure introduced in that same historical year.

So, after a tumultuous arrival, I quickly recovered from what threatened to be a quick exit. As life unfolded Mama often wondered aloud about this propitious turn of events; was Alice simply a kind, caring, and sympathetic midwife – or was she a prophet in disguise?

Chapter 2
Unlikely Farmers

The only thing more improbable than my coming into the family when I did was that Harry and Helen Beck, a Jewish couple from Brooklyn, by way of Eastern Europe, would own a dairy farm in upstate, New York.

Who are those people who bought the old dairy farm on Route 107, they wondered. They sure don't look like they come from around here; can hardly understand what they say.

The farmers, hired hands and merchants who lived and worked in the area would soon get to know their new neighbors as well as their soon to arrive new additions: Benny, born less than a year after they settled in, followed by Shirley, two short years later.

The new nuclear family lived in a big old farmhouse on 186 acres near the village of Delanson about seven miles from Schoharie in upstate Schenectady County, New York. The property stretched across route 7, a major highway. It wasn't unusual for traffic to come to a complete stop when their cows crossed the road to graze. When the cattle weren't holding up the wheels of progress, Babe and Bess, the family's two horses put the brakes on automobile traffic as they pulled one of the few remaining horse and buggies into town.

Benny recalled the house through eight year-old eyes. *"It had a big front porch shaded by a large Poplar tree. Close to the edge of the shade of the tree, there was an overgrown rose-bush with fragrant, light pink flowers, and a bed of Peonies that must have withstood twenty cold winters. Nearby, a water pump stood on a wet wood platform that led to the kitchen sink where a pitcher pump with a handle completed the plumbing system. There was a good-sized, black, cast iron stove with four removable lids on top. Below the oven was a nickel-plated molding where you could warm your feet in the morning while the stove heated up. Out the back door was the wood shed; it had a dirt floor and the aroma of decaying sawdust and bark. About twenty yards behind the wood shed was the unpainted outhouse."*

It didn't take long before it became obvious that raising a young family and operating a dairy farm was a lot different from tending one or two cows, a horse, a few chickens, and a vegetable garden for family consumption as Daddy had done as a young boy. So too was his vision of sitting under a tree reading James Hilton's "Lost Horizon," quickly dashed. The reality was that he didn't have enough time to complete his chores let alone peruse the verse of Shakespeare. For Mama, instead of an adventure, her worst fears about Daddy's idealistic dreams, lack of entrepreneurial and agricultural experience, not to mention insufficient working capital quickly materialized.

Again, I think Benny said it best from his point of view as a young child: *"There were about twenty cows; maybe ten milked by hand every morning. One cow named Benson was brindle and white. She was acquired from a neighbor named Benson and I wondered why his cows were milked by machines and Daddy milked by hand. The next farm down the road was Clifford Westfall's. He cut hay with a tractor mower and raked with two side delivery rakes pulled by a tractor. Daddy used a dump rake, which took twice as long. Daddy had a hay loader but didn't use it because you needed two people to operate it, one to drive the tractor and another on the wagon to build the load. Daddy raked the hay into "hay cocks". Two horses, Babe and Bess, moved the wagon ahead and stopped while Daddy pitched the hay cocks into the wagon with a long-handled, three-prong fork. When the load covered about six feet of the wagon floor, many times Daddy put Shirley and Benny on top of the hay for a fun ride up the barn bridge into the barn."*

In the face of many obstacles, long days of back-breaking labor, the proverbial blood sweat and tears, Daddy tried hard to make a go of the farm. He did his best, rising early in the morning to milk cows, bail hay, tend the animals and the land, and mend fences, all with a minimum of help. Mom did her share as well to maintain the house, feed the chickens, gather fresh eggs, cultivate corn and potato crops, care for two young children, and cook three meals every day for the family and hired hands.

Some of her early culinary attempts drew strange responses. One day, for instance, two workers sat motionless looking at bowls of red liquid with boiled potatoes placed before them; they exchanged questioning glances and did not attempt to eat it. Sensing their apprehension, Mama explained: "it's beet soup, very popular in Russia." Finally, one man nervously picked up a spoonful, took a sip, grimaced, pushed the plate away, and stated in no uncertain terms: "Helen, no more beet soup!"

They preferred more familiar dishes like steak and potatoes, pork shops or sausages perhaps. Handling pork was, however, repulsive to Mama. All of her life she had been taught that it was forbidden by Jewish dietary laws clearly stated in the bible. She never ate it or any other forbidden food including shell fish except for one unforgettable experience. Soon after she arrived in the U.S., her Americanized cousins took her out to a restaurant, ordered her a shrimp salad sandwich and told her it was tuna. After she took a few bites, they burst out laughing:

"Helen, do you know you are eating shrimp?"

Her response was to run to the ladies room and throw it up. She was angry with them for years to come.

After the borscht incident she made it her business to learn how to prepare sausages, bacon and ham with eggs, and pork loin for the hungry farm hands.

The family quickly became a part of the community and made good friends. Benny wrote about how they helped each other:

"At harvest time, for silo filling, thrashing and bailing, some willing and able neighbors showed up and made short work of these big jobs. They brought equipment, horses-and-wagons, and their wives who had lunch and socialized."

Notwithstanding the kindness of the community and Mom's and Dad's best efforts, it was a losing battle. Operating costs grew out of proportion to income. Ever increasing expensive sanitary regulations were forced on dairy farmers while prices paid for milk and byproducts did not keep up with added expenditures.

During the fur season from late December through mid-summer, Daddy worked weekdays in New York to supplement the family income. He came home every other weekend; life for Mama was particularly tough. She was forced to manage the farm, the hands and two young children all by herself. She couldn't easily reach Daddy because communications were still archaic. Aunt Molly, with whose family he stayed, didn't have a phone in her Brooklyn apartment and the phone on the farm was a shared line.

After almost eleven years of hardship, hard work and anxiety, they huddled in front of the old barn together – Daddy, Benny, Shirley and Mama – her belly swollen with a twenty-six week old fetus (me) in her womb – as their home and livelihood came under the auctioneer's hammer.

First on the block were their much-loved horses Babe and Bess; next the bull, cows and other livestock, who had become Benny's and Shirley's pets; next came the tractor, wagon and tools. Finally the hammer came down on the land along with the big old barn and the family home.

Mama couldn't believe how her fortunes had changed in the years since she left her native land and the life she had made for herself here in the U.S.

Warm heartfelt hugs from friends, neighbors and townspeople could not console her or slow the tears that stained her tired face. Daddy held the kids close to him and stoically tried not to cry for their sakes. The loss of their first home, impoverished as it was, represented the end of a dream.

Chapter 3
Digging into Our Roots

Was Dad's dream just that, an impossible flight of fancy? Perhaps. Prior to purchasing the farm, his only agricultural experience came from tending the family's small menagerie of a few cows, some chickens and a vegetable patch that yielded enough milk, eggs, fruits and vegetables for their own consumption.

The scant knowledge we have about our paternal ancestors and their journey from Biblical lands to Europe to America starts in 1882 when Zalman Bak or Bac (the family wasn't sure which) and Suzan Rebecca Gelaubter married and settled in their hometown of Kosmacz, Galicia in the province of Stanislav in the then Austria-Hungary Empire.

Their home was situated on a small piece of land at the foot of the Carpathian Mountains that run through Eastern Europe. Daddy was the fourth of six children born to Zalman and Suzan between 1883 and 1903, including Max, Ida, and Molly who preceded Daddy and Nettie and Dora who followed him. Daddy's official given name was Herchel. His family, however, called him "Alta" (Yiddish for "old"). His parents like many of their peers were superstitious and felt the additional name would ward off his namesake's fate of an early death.

Dora and Nettie told stories of how when Dad was as young as eleven or twelve, neighbors turned to him for help with daily activities, such as record keeping and written correspondence; this despite the fact that his formal education ended with the sixth grade. Under the rule of Emperor Franz Joseph, Austria was one of the few countries in the region where there were equal rights that allowed Jewish children to attend school.

Though the regime was more forward thinking than others, opportunities for Jews to enhance their social status were extremely limited. This along with a bad economy drove many Galician Jews from their homeland. Between 1881 and 1910 the United States naturalized more than three million Austrian immigrants, of which over a quarter million were from Galicia.

In 1906 Grandpa Zalman and then twenty-three year-old Uncle Max joined the exodus of emigrants who left home to establish new homesteads in America, leaving Dad to take care of the things back home. Folklore has it that they were not permitted to enter on their first try. Reasons, fact or fiction, range from illness to Grandpa being wanted for assaulting someone back home. In any event, they went, instead, to England for several years where they learned the fur business.

On their second attempt around 1908, they were admitted to the United States at Ellis Island, New York. It was there that they acquired their American names, Solomon and Max Back; immigration agents often misunderstood names because of accents and varying dialects. As a result, they phonetically dubbed refugees with similar sounding names. In other cases, the immigrants themselves changed their names to more American sounding ones. Either way, the name recorded at Ellis Island became official for life.

The father and son established a home base in the East New York section of Brooklyn and soon started a business in Manhattan's fur district where they manufactured mouton coats and accessories. "Mouton," French for sheep is sheepskin processed to resemble beaver or seal fur; for years it was a popular affordable alternative to more expensive mink, sable and Persian lamb among other furs reserved for the well to do.

In 1911, three years after he arrived here, Grandpa Solomon sent for the rest of the family, Grandma, Dad and his sisters. When they disembarked at Ellis Island the immigration agent altered their surname as they did with Solomon and Max; this time, however, they changed "Bak" to "Beck." Thus the family has two surnames; our grandparents and uncle's family went by "Back," while Dad and his sisters by "Beck." Thus we have cousins of various degrees with either name.

When the family arrived, Grandpa and Max took them to their apartment. Dad didn't talk much about the details but from what I gather it was a pretty standard railroad apartment, basically a straight line of rooms, one after another where you walked through one to get to the next. Grandma and grandpa shared a bedroom room as did the four girls and Dad bunked with Max. I don't recall if their bathroom was outside or they shared an inside one with other tenants in the building.

Dad joined Grandpa and Max in their established business where he quickly learned how to operate a sewing machine, buy and season pelts, cut, and sell coats to the trade.

Ida and Molly took jobs in factories, Nettie and Dora, ages 12 and eight respectively were enrolled in elementary school. Like millions of other immigrants, the family could not speak English. Grandpa and Max, like most adults in their position, had attended classes at night in the local elementary school. Upon their arrival, Dad, Ida and Molly did the same. Dad was full-grown at eighteen and felt uncomfortable in the small seats so he quickly dropped out.

Instead, most evenings after work, he taught himself to read in the public library. He used translations in Hebrew and German, both of which he knew how to read and write. He somehow matched the translations to an English version of the Declaration of Independence and later to American history books. He not only learned the language but before long he managed to read and understand the New York Times better than anyone I ever knew including myself. Soon he read it every day and became well versed in world affairs and a variety of other subjects.

Dad was not happy. He disliked the city, apartment living (he quickly dubbed apartment buildings "chicken coops unfit for humans) and the fur business. The factory was hot and confining. Dust and fur hung in the still air like thousands of gray and brown snow flakes. He longed to be back in the open spaces of his homeland – back to nature, animals, and the land.

There was, however, no going back. The world he left behind was quickly transformed. Under the pressure of revolutions throughout Europe the entire region underwent myriad geographical changes. In 1936 Aunt Dora tried to obtain information about the land the family owned. She was advised by the Consulate General of the Republic of Poland, of which the region had become a part, that there had been two towns called "Kosmacz" in the former Galicia, that they were apparently situated in two different counties in the same province, and it appeared neither existed anymore.

Still, the little we know from Dad, his sisters and Mama, who had many conversations with Grandpa, offers at least some insight into our paternal roots – and the origins of a few familial characteristics that seem to have prevailed through the generations.

Chapter 4
Mama's Origins

When it comes to Mama's biological background, we have little to no information. She was adopted immediately after birth by her maternal aunt and uncle and had almost no familiarity with her natural nuclear family.

We know that her given name was Chana *(ch" is pronounced as if you're clearing phlegm from your throat and the first "a" as a short "o")*. She was the third child of a mother who was widowed while pregnant with her. Her father died young (Mama did not know the cause of death), leaving her mother to care for her young son and daughter by working as a street peddler.

Mama was born in July 1903, almost ten years after Daddy's birth, some 1,000 miles away, in southern Russia which was part of the same troubled region of the world.

She had the good fortune to be raised by her mother's sister Pia and her husband Nissim Kessler, the only parents she knew and loved. They raised her in an affluent home adorned with crystal chandeliers, expensive wood furniture, silk drapes, elegant china and linens. Hired help tended to the house. While a governess tended to her basic needs, Mama's parents doted on her, giving her everything money could buy – from expensive clothing, jewelry, books – to an abundance of love and affection. She was an only child - one they thought they would never have.

Many of her memories had to do with her father's keen entrepreneurial aptitude that made their lifestyle possible. She was taken by the creative ways he overcame objections in the sale of coats.

"You say this is too heavy?" he would ask placing the coat on the prospective buyer's arm, making sure his hand was carefully placed under the garment to add a little buoyancy.

"It's light like a feather. Any lighter it won't be warm!"

For the customer who thought the same coat was too light to be warm, he reversed his approach, placing his hands on top of the garment and applying just a little pressure to assure the prospective buyer that a coat as heavy is this would surely be warm.

Mama's recounting of her father's sale of men's suits sounded much like a joke that circulated for many years about the gyrations a customer was put through until he was grotesquely contorted by the time the salesman declared:

"Now that's how a suit should fit!"

Her father's entrepreneurial skills and antics offered Mama many luxuries and above all the chance at an education. Most Jewish children in Eastern Europe were not allowed to go to school and many non-Jews were unable to attend for financial reasons. As a result of her parents' wealth, Mama was graduated from "Gymnasioa," the equivalent of our high school and the highest level of learning available for most students, regardless of their faith.

Getting an education was just one of many difficulties of growing up in Russia during the early 1900's, a period of almost constant war. The first ten years of the reign of Czar Nicholas II were relatively uneventful; by the time Mama was two, however, the quiet ended. In the revolution of 1905 government troops fired on workers marching to protest against poor working conditions. Hundreds of people were killed and or wounded earning that day the designation of "Bloody Sunday." Although Nicholas had nothing to do with this action – he actually expressed sorrow about it – the workers' leaders denounced him as the "sole murderer of the Russian people." The events of that day are considered by historians to be key elements that led to the eventual Russian Revolution of 1917. But first there was World War I in 1914.

Add to war, the terrible atrocities perpetrated on Jews just because of their religion. Pogroms (riots against Jews) that began in the Middle Ages when they were blamed for the crucifixion of Jesus Christ, remained prevalent throughout Europe.

Mama never forgot how she and a few friends were accosted by a group of Cossacks on their way home from school when she was about twelve. The big burly young men with smirks on their faces handed them shovels.

"Dig here" the meanest looking one said pointing to a spot on the ground.

"Keep digging," they taunted. "Make it comfortable. This will be your final resting place."

Gripped by fear, sweat streaming from her pores, she obeyed. Finally she managed to pay them off with a few rubles.

"OK" they said, "be on your way and make sure you don't walk by this way tomorrow."

The would-be murderers walked away, patting each other on the back and laughing.

Such unacceptable behavior, governmental corruption, the reactionary policies of Tsar Nicholas II, catastrophic Russian losses in World War I and economic hardship, together continued to make life less and less bearable.

Then in 1917, when the Russian Revolution began, the Bolsheviks (communists) wanted complete government control of everything. Millions of Russian farmers of all faiths were killed because they refused to turn their property over to the government. Under communism, private business became illegal. This and the ultimate communist victory made Mama and her family subject to the resulting violence, cruelty, repression, exploitation and abuse.

Our grandfather, for example, was caught selling clothing, the only way he knew to make a living. He was jailed, beaten, and fed only enough food to subsist. Mama described her fear as she tentatively walked into the jail – under five feet tall, stiff legged, dressed in fine clothes, looking up at the tall scary looking uniformed guards – to negotiate with them as to just how many rubles it would take to free her dad.

At one point the Bolsheviks took over the family's home for their headquarters.

Fed up with the abuse of power, oppression and war, thousands of Russians fled to the United States, South America, Palestine (Israel in 1948), and other countries around the world. Mama's best friend urged her to leave. Mama begged her parents to come away with her.

"Please, let's go before they kill us," she pleaded.

"You go. We are too old to start over," her father told her.

"But they will kill you if you stay here."

"What will be, will be," her mother agreed with her husband.

"We can't run away from our home, not at this time in our lives. You are young. You have your whole life ahead of you. You go – find a better life."

Finally, in 1919, at the age of 16, after much soul searching, Mama and her best friend decided to go to America; at the last minute her friend decided to go to Palestine where a new Jewish state was just beginning to be built.

Mama left her parents behind and joined the throngs of immigrants to America, the "Land of Milk and Honey." On her way to the port in Hamburg, Germany, Mama somehow ended up in Romania. The details were never clear. However, she often told the story of when she disembarked from a train at a stop there. A young man offered to hold her bags while she sought information about continuing her trip. Minutes later when she looked for him to reclaim her belongings he was gone. She lost all of her money and mementos her parents had given her. A young couple at the depot witnessed what happened and took her in to live with them and their young child.

She found herself sleeping on a hard table in their single room. They all shared a single slice of bread and a piece of herring a day. Mama experienced abject poverty for the first time. She also picked up quite a bit of the language and culture while she was there. After giving serious consideration to returning home, her parents sent her money to continue her voyage.

With these fresh resources, she immediately reimbursed the young family that had given her so much that money could not repay. She then purchased tickets and finally boarded another train to Hamburg where she embarked on a ship to the U.S.

Onboard, hordes of immigrants crowded together in the steerage compartment. Food, lavatories and bathing facilities were few and the seas were rough for most of the crossing. Mom described a chaotic scene of young children screaming from hunger and illness, the agony of aged and infirm men and women, many of whom died along the way, and people of all ages, including herself, heaving all over the ship. The stench was unbearable.

On the sixteenth morning she heard a commotion on deck. Passengers cried, laughed and hugged each other when they spotted the majestic Statue of Liberty. At last they were about to set foot on a new land where people of all faiths and nationalities lived in peace and freedom. Most had endured myriad hardships in their quest to reach this destination.

In the spring of 1921, Chana arrived at Ellis Island where she became Helen Kessler. Four young cousins whom she had never seen before met her and took her to live with them in their small walk-up apartment in Brooklyn, New York. No, the streets were not paved with gold as she had expected. However she would no longer suffer persecution because of her ethnicity or be abused by a corrupt government. She welcomed a lifestyle free of oppression and during the next six years acclimated herself to life as an American. At the same time she was disappointed at the reality of her crowded living conditions, relatively low economic status and realization of how much she wished her parents were here with her.

Still, she liked being totally responsible for herself for the first time in her life; she worked hard as a floor person in a hat factory, paid her share of the rent and was soon able to purchase fashionable clothing. In the evenings after work, she went to school to learn English and began to see herself as part of the American dream.

Ironically, Mama's independence began the same year the Russian Revolution ended. The Bolsheviks were victorious. Unfortunately, Mama who had kept in touch with her parents, lost contact without knowing what happened to them then or during World War II. This was a source of regret and pain for the rest of her life.

I often think about Mama and so many other brave heroes who set out alone for far away places where they did not speak or understand the language; where they had no idea of what to expect or how they would survive. Their courage, daring and spirit truly made America what it is, and bestowed upon us — their descendents — the good fortune to be citizens of the greatest country in the world.

Extensive records have been kept in places like Yad Vashem in Jerusalem and Ellis Island about the hordes of Europeans who were driven from their homelands in the early 1900s. I have visited both locations and tried to search their vast databases without success.

Regrettably, we have no documents — passports, evidence of the ships that brought them to our shores, even actual names — which makes a successful exploration of their early lives impossible.

Chapter 5
Their American Dream

Sometime in early 1927 these two people from similar, yet different backgrounds and with widely divergent ideas for their futures, were introduced to each other.

Mom was getting comfortable in her new life. Yet, like many young women, she had mixed emotions; on one hand she wanted to become more independent; to be able to move out of the apartment she shared with her cousins into one of her own; on the other, she wished to meet "Mr. Right," a tall, dark, handsome Romeo who would sweep her off of her feet, marry her and together they would live the "American dream."

Dad at thirty-five, felt it was about time he settled down too. He, however, still held onto his fantasy of living in rural America – surrounded by wide open spaces, animals and lots of trees under which he could recline and read to his hearts delight – preferably the poetry of Walt Whitman.

He was quite pleased when he first met Mom – petite at five feet-one inch tall, one hundred and ten pounds, a full head of curly, strawberry blond hair and big brown eyes – he noticed that she scrutinized him from head-to-toe in a single sweep.

Mom was not as taken by him. he was anything but the towering, bronzed, attractive partner she had imagined; just five foot-ten, with a fair complexion, once red hair already graying and receding, and sky blue eyes as opposed to the deep dark mysterious wells of wisdom she had visualized.

Yet something attracted her. Compared to other men she had met, she found him to be more worldly, quite knowledgeable and pleasant to be with. They courted for a year, during which time they went to movies, met with friends, talked about their pasts and their hopes for the future. He told her about his desire to some day own a farm; she shrugged it off as an implausible fantasy.

In March 1928, a year after they met, they married in a small ceremony in Dad's parents' living room.

Grandpa Solomon, keenly aware of Dad's dream, quickly helped him buy a large dairy farm in upstate New York. Mom was leery about the prospects of such a move. After already having overcome so much, she submerged her doubts and fears. She convinced herself that a totally new way of life could turn out to be an exciting adventure. So off they went to live happily ever after.

Soon after Mom and Dad settled in Uncle Max who was living in Brooklyn with his wife and three sons bought a large spread nearby.

Both Dad and Max continued to go to New York and stay with Grandpa and Grandma or Aunt Molly during the fur season to earn some extra cash.

Max's three sons, Eddie, Abe, and Sydney were teenagers. Benny thought that was one reason Max's farm was more successful. Dad had started his family on the farm and never reached the point where the kids could help with the chores like Max's three sons did. Max died at the farm in his early forties of a sudden heart attack. Eddie, his oldest son (and the oldest of my first cousins) married his high school sweetheart, Alice; ultimately they took over the farm and raised their family there. Max's wife moved back to Brooklyn as did Abe and Sydney where they married and started families of their own.

Chapter 6
Quaker Street, the Village

After they lost the farm, the family relocated to Quaker Street, the sister village to Delanson. They lived in a small apartment above a store in this historic village that dates back to 1893. Their new accommodations were a far cry from the big old colonial, the only home Benny and Shirley had ever known. They missed running around the house, the barn and the grounds and wished they could still be near the animals. Mama and Daddy, too, missed the fresh milk, eggs and ambiance.

Mama, now in the late months of her pregnancy continued to grow exponentially as I grew in her womb. It was a difficult time for her to be alone with two growing kids and Daddy was rarely home to comfort and help her. He was spending most of his time in New York, working in any union shop that needed help and looking for a place to move the family.

In the last few years the family fur business in New York City, where he had worked during the fur season, had closed. Grandpa Solomon had passed away from uric poisoning that resulted presumably from a prostate condition when he was in his mid sixties. Uncle Max, too, passed away from a sudden heart attack in his forties.

Daddy came home every few weeks to spend as much time as he could with the family. Fortunately he was there when I decided to make my grand entrance. After the trauma of my birth ended, Daddy introduced Benny and Shirley to their new baby sister. Benny was thrilled but Shirley — not so much.

"Uch! She's ugly; She doesn't look anything like Nancy Jo," she shouted.

"She's only a baby. In no time she'll be three years old just like Nancy Jo. You'll be able to play with her and help take care of her," Dad tried to appease her.

"You promised me a baby sister like Nancy Jo," she bellowed. "I wanna go see Nancy Jo," she cried.

She put some clothing in a bag and headed for the door; she was running away from home. Unable to calm her down, Daddy who did not own a car, walked her to Nancy Jo's house about a quarter mile away. Her legs were too short to negotiate the foot and a half of snow so Daddy threw her in front of him every few feet until they arrived at their destination.

Within hours the phone rang. Shirley was homesick and still crying. Nancy Jo's Dad was kind enough to drive her back despite the terrible driving conditions. I wish I could say she eventually got over it but I don't think she ever did.

To this day when I meet people who come from that area, I am always surprised that they are familiar with the Village of Quaker Street; located on Route 7, still a main thoroughfare in the Albany metropolitan area.

Chapter 7
Living Vicariously on the Farm

After I listened to reminiscences of the farm over and over again, at once happy and harrowing, I felt like I was actually alongside Benny and Shirley as they climbed up the silo, played in the hay loft and skated around the inside of the house. But I was too young to be a part of their lives at the time. Close in age, growing up in a sparsely populated community, they were each other's primary playmates, confidants and nemeses.

They were inseparable until Benny started school. It was in a one-room schoolhouse with 8-10 other children from neighboring farms, almost all at different grade levels. While Benny progressed quickly, mostly by listening in on lessons directed at the older kids, Shirley, only three years old, ached to be with him.

She acted out through increasingly frequent fits of temper; she did not yet speak in sentences. Mama worried that there was something wrong with her. When she turned four and still didn't speak, Mama, Shirley at her side, told Mrs. Lettuce about her fears.

A gentle, experienced teacher and mentor for many years, Mrs. Lettuce looked at the short, slender, forlorn little girl looking down at the ground.

"Shirley," she asked "would you like to come to school with Benny?" Shirley's big eyes opened wide as she shyly shook her head yes.

When the bus arrived home after her first day, she ran off shouting:

"I started to talk today! I started to talk today!"

In the retelling of this story Benny always added "and she hasn't shut up since."

He dubbed her "the actress" in part, because she could turn her emotions on and off like a water spigot. If she wanted something, she tucked her chin down, looked up through the tops of her eyes and fluttered her lashes. If that didn't work, she lied down on the floor and went into a kicking and screaming tantrum. The instant she got her way, she was back to her old charming self. Her acting prowess was also the subject of an oft repeated story about her lead role in a school play in which a girl had the flu . . . Shirley's big line was: "her hands flew, her legs flew, her head flew, everything flew."

Despite the anticipated sibling bickering, they were always there for each other. When Benny accidentally tumbled off the silo which he wasn't allowed to climb, Shirley was right there to run to the house for help; when he came home from the hospital with his arm in a cast, she wanted one too. The two were inseparable. On cold nights they slept together to stay warm.

Benny was, from what I understand, rather quiet and contemplative even as a young child. I don't recall many details about his escapades on the farm. He did talk about a particularly exciting and unforgettable July 4th trip into town with Dad. He recounted how Dad bought him his first "big-boy" pants and the excitement of seeing a marching band for the first time.

Even in face of the hardships, both Benny and Shirley had indelible memories of the farm. So much so that Benny never adjusted to city living; he gravitated toward and was happiest in agricultural settings. As for Shirley, while on the surface she adapted to urban life, in the end she settled on a thirty-acre farm forty miles west of Knoxville, Tennessee where the family owned a few horses.

No matter how much I tried to be a part of the family, I was an outsider – an interloper in a very private world they shared before I came along – a place that began with so much hope and ended with the demise of a dream.

Chapter 8
Urban Homestead

In November 1939 Mama — with the three of us, a few suitcases of clothing, and a head spinning with anticipation and apprehension — boarded a bus to New York City.

Family folklore has it that I cried if anyone so much as looked at me, and yet, after not seeing Daddy for most of my eight months of life I went right into his waiting arms to a new way of life that awaited the whole family.

The small apartment on east 181st Street overlooked Bronx Park, an urban oasis with over seven hundred acres of grass, trees, and walking paths, a bucolic setting that became the center of our new reality.

This vast pastoral setting, however, couldn't counteract the culture shock for Benny and Shirley. The change from the farmhouse and even the Quaker Street apartment, with abundant space, to the cramped apartment with families living next to them, above them, below them along the dark narrow hallways and stairways that they cautiously navigated was staggering.

From their one-room schoolhouse with eight-to-ten students scattered from kindergarten through eighth grade, to P.S. 67, a four-story brick building with almost a thousand kids, thirty to a classroom, from kindergarten to sixth grade.

From the horse and buggy into town to a walk to East 180th Street, two blocks from home lined with stores — groceries, fresh fruit and a store that sold only candy. They never saw so many people in one place, let alone ice cream carts and trucks that came right to your door. That part wasn't hard to get used to, nor was suddenly having lots of playmates.

The streets quickly became their primary source of entertainment. Despite their early apprehension, Benny quickly began playing stickball in the streets and Shirley jumped rope, played hopscotch and bouncing ball games on the sidewalks of the Bronx.

Almost immediately the family also became fixtures at the park and zoo. I can still smell the roasted peanuts as we approached the West Farms gate from when I was about five years old on. For a nickel, the vendor handed us a small brown paper bag, the top skillfully folded. The feel of the warm shell, the crunch and taste linger in my psyche.

I'd hold a few peanuts out to the llamas and their warm fuzzy snouts on my palms sent shivers up my spine; the elephants curled their trunks into an "S" pointing two giant nostrils in my direction for me to pitch whole peanuts into; then they curled the trunk back and deposited the nuts in their mouths. We tossed whole fish to the dark spotted, whiskered critters with big noses and large sad eyes during feeding time at the seal exhibit; some sprawled lazily on rocks and opened their mouths, while others leapt to catch the food in mid-air.

There were lions, monkeys, giraffes – animals of every stripe and color. Many wandered in outdoor fenced-in pens while others were behind glass in cement and brick buildings. The level of excitement, ambiance, lighting, and odors varied from exhibit to exhibit. The stench of the elephant house still lingers in my minds nose.

Throughout spring and summer, we joined friends and neighbors in the Park. We strolled the paths until we found a nice spot; spread our sandwiches and drinks and picnicked. While the adults talked, my friends and I rolled down the grassy hills, the bumpier the better. Occasionally we rented a row boat from the boat house at the base of the waterfall and paddled around a small section of the Bronx River. Smaller parks and playgrounds dotted every neighborhood.

On religious holidays we donned new clothing and took pictures sitting on the fountain, rocks and grass.

Chapter 9
Window to the World

Less than two years after the big move to the city we packed up again and moved south, albeit only about eight blocks. We traded the view of the park for an additional bedroom so Benny and Shirley each had their own rooms; I still slept between Mommy and Daddy.

By now Benny had already graduated from P.S. 67 and was attending Junior High School 118 which he had started before we moved. Shirley, having graduated from P.S.67 the June before we moved was enrolled in P.S.6 just two blocks from home.

Yours truly, still the family's displaced person stayed home with Mommy and watched the world through the living room window. On rainy days, we watched the drops slide down the window while Mommy recited the old nursery rhyme "rain, rain, go away, come again some other day."

I watched people come and go from the stores across the street — at Manny's candy store they picked up a pack of cigarettes, or a newspaper, or sat at the counter and drank a "two-cents plain," otherwise known as seltzer or carbonated water. I waited for Shirley and her school friends to come home for lunch. They'd eat fast and then converge at Manny's where they pointed at their choices from scores of confections displayed in the glass showcases.

"I'll take one "Mary Jane," a sheet of buttons, three caramels, and two of those chocolate things" a little girl would say, putting a nickel or a few pennies on the counter before running back to school. At 3:05 they returned for a malted and a long pretzel. Many opted for a chocolate egg cream that contained neither egg nor cream; it is made with a few tablespoons of chocolate syrup from the fountain and an equal amount of milk, topped off with seltzer that gushed from the fountain as the soda jerk briskly mixed until the creamy white head flowed over the edges of the glass.

Mama had an arrangement with Manny to give Benny and Shirley as many malteds or pretzels as they wanted, but not a lot of junk. She brought an egg in each morning for him to put in Shirley's malted because she was very thin and presumably undernourished.

Men went in and out of Frank's Barber Shop next door. I learned later that they didn't always get a haircut and a shave; Frank was the friendly neighborhood bookie. One wintry weekend morning as I gazed out at the snow I saw a commotion in his doorway; it turned out that a homeless man had frozen to death overnight.

Most of what I saw through my private prism, however, was positive. I giggled at the sight of Benny playing stickball, his chunky body making for an awkward gait as he ran the bases. His friends nicknamed him "Boom-Boom," an acronym for his initials "BB" coupled with his less than stellar ability to hit the ball. To be fair he had a late start in learning the game and was therefore at an unfair disadvantage.

One Friday afternoon in late fall Mom looked out and didn't see Benny playing with his friends. She ran downstairs and nervously asked the other kids: "Where's Benny?"

"The Rabbi called him into the Synagogue," they replied.

Mama burst into the building to see Benny turning off lights as the Rabbi stood beside him.

"What are you doing here, what's going on?" she shouted.

The Rabbi responded:

"It's sundown so I asked him to turn off the lights for us."

"What!" she exclaimed. You're making him your 'Shabbas Goy;' he's a Jewish boy!"

A bright shade of crimson crept across he Rabbi's face. The term "Shabbas Goy" (Sabbath non-Jew) refers to the latter carrying out chores prohibited for Jews on the Sabbath which begins on Friday evening at sundown.

There was no reason for the Rabbi to know Benny was Jewish; he was, after all, out playing ball after the start of the Sabbath and the family never introduced themselves or attended Synagogue.

"I'm so sorry" he apologized "I didn't know; I never saw him before, or you, in the Synagogue. It looks like he should be getting ready for a Bar Mitzvah. Where does he go for lessons?"

The Rabbi was very perceptive. Benny was about to turn thirteen in a few months but had been reluctant to go to Hebrew School.

"He doesn't want to go to Hebrew School," Mama said.

"No Hebrew school, no Bar Mitzvah," the Rabbi exclaimed in disbelief. "Please come in with your husband and Benny on Monday. We have to talk about this."

They did. Benny enrolled in Hebrew school but was quickly disillusioned about not understanding what he was being taught. Bar Mitzvah classes consist largely of memorizing biblical passages from the bible and related commentary in Hebrew. Most often the boys (more recently girls too) are not taught the literal translations and are therefore ignorant of what they are reciting to the congregation.

"I told you, I'm not going to stand up in front of people and chant words I don't understand!" Benny declared.

Daddy then made arrangements to continue preparation privately, one-on-one, thinking Benny might understand more of what he was going to have to recite; this too turned out not to be the case. In the end, Benny refused to continue; his thirteenth birthday came and went without a Bar Mitzvah. Not a problem; Mama and Daddy, themselves disillusioned with religion and believing assimilation was the safest way to prevent repetition of the atrocities they suffered, relented.

I continued to watch life through my window. It was through that same lens that I imagined that I would someday be like my big sister, Shirley and jump rope, play Potsy and bouncing ball games with my own friends. I was mesmerized by how the big girls jumped in to the turning clothesline and kept jumping to a rhyme without getting tangled up in the rope before leaping out. In double-dutch, they jumped into two ropes turning toward each other simultaneously. I marveled, too, at how they repeatedly bounced the ball. For each letter of the alphabet, and any word starting with that letter, they bounced the ball under one lifted leg while they stood on the other leg and recited:

"A" my name is Alice and my husband's name is Al we come from Alabama and we sell Apples. "B" my name is . . ."

During the war, windows were integral to our national security. On many a tranquil evening while listening to the radio, a wailing siren sounded making everyone jump; it was as if the sky was screaming. Mommy and Daddy quickly turned the radio and lights off and drew the shades. I followed behind and tugged the shades away from the windows a little to see out, but I could barely make out the men wearing white hats walking up and down the street below.

At three or four years old I had lots of questions about what was happening.

I didn't understand that we were at war; that blackouts were a precaution to prevent enemy aircraft from seeing where the big cities were and possibly targeting them with bombing raids. I didn't know that our neighbors, who I saw marching back and forth, were air raid wardens who played a big part in the country's civil defense program by enforcing the rules during blackouts. The slightest hint of light coming from an apartment window, a car light or a lit cigarette on the supposedly unoccupied streets drew a stern reprimand. When the drill ended the all-clear siren sounded and everything went back to normal.

Windows contributed to community life. They were crucial conduits for exchanging news and gossip, for keeping an eye out for family or for friends calling for each other. Mothers looked after their kids, scolded them – and threw snacks, sweaters and wrapped coins for the candy store to them – through the window.

Several times a year, people tossed worn clothing through the window to a man who made a living by selling it for a few pennies; every so often he went through the courts and backyards yelling:

"I cash clothes."

From time to time a violinist serenaded us in the same way; listeners dropped a few coins through the window in appreciation.

For many, the window was like television which wouldn't arrive for another three or four years; it wasn't unusual to see people just sitting and looking out the window for hours at a time.

On hot summer nights it was our air conditioning; we opened all the windows wide and if we were lucky enough to have two in one room we had cross ventilation.

Today you rarely see anyone gazing through a window, throwing things out of one or talking to someone via anything as simple as a window. With air conditioning, television, computers, cell phones, I-phones, I-pads – the once versatile window has lost its utility. I often wonder if we as a society lost something too.

Chapter 10
My Big Bang

The "big bang" theory hypothesizes that the universe began ten-to-fifteen billion years ago with a random cosmic explosion creating the stars, galaxies, and the planets, including earth by hurling matter and energy in all directions. The impeccable order that followed the "big bang," sometimes referred to as "intelligent design," somehow seems contrary to the disorder and disarray one would expect from such a blast.

While it did not involve an explosion, I experienced a similar seemingly random, instantaneous realization of my existence at about four years of age. I found myself sitting on the stone stoop of our building on 178th Street. It was as if, like the universe, I suddenly materialized out of nowhere.

Many of my memories seem to precede my big bang and appear as foggy vignettes making it difficult to remember which came when. Nor am I certain which were actual experiences and which I may think I recall because of stories I have repeatedly heard.

For example, somewhere in the recesses of my mind's eye there are images of Mama using rationing stamps. During World War II, the purchases of sugar, gum, canned goods and other products that were in short supply because they were in some way used in the war effort were limited accordingly. If you knew the grocer well, however, you could get some extras. And, who didn't know the grocer; he was also the neighborhood banker. Ours was Mr. Checknowski and we like most families ran a tab with him. He kept a careful accounting in a dog-eared, black-marble covered composition book.

I also can picture the butcher, Mr. Lobel in his blood stained white coat with whom Mama ran a running account too.

In another internal snapshot, Mama is carrying me up the narrow stairwell. She stops on the second floor to visit with Mrs. Ziddick outside her door; I can't be older than three. They speak in a foreign language – not Yiddish. I later found out that it was Ukrainian which Mama had learned on her journey to America. Other neighbors also appear in my vague visions. None are of children my age. They are of Shirley's and Benny's friends.

One image after my "big bang" is quite clear. It is of a night Benny's buddy Paul came by. Mama and Daddy had gone to see Margaret O'Brien in a romantic comedy. I don't know which one, but it had to be very special because Mama and Daddy never went out. At Benny's urging and a promise to take care of Shirley and me, Mama finally worked up the courage to leave us alone; it seemed safe enough. Benny was fourteen, Shirley twelve, making me four.

All went well for the first hour or so. Then Paul yelled up at the window to Benny to come down and toss a football with him. *They would stay in front of the house; what harm could come of that,* Benny reasoned.

"You can't go. Mama left you in charge." Shirley whined.

"I'll be right downstairs – just holler if you need me."

"No, you can't go and leave me alone with Susie."

He ignored her plea and left. She yelled out the window for him to come back up. Embarrassed, he went upstairs to try to talk some sense into her. What ensued was like a scene from "The Bad Seed." She started jumping up and down, crying, and screaming. That's when we heard a real big bang.

Benny and Shirley froze. I cried. The crash sounded like it came from the apartment below. Next we heard a loud knock on the door. Benny hesitantly opened it. The downstairs neighbor stood staring at him, red faced, furious:

"Where's your father?" he demanded.

"He's not home, can I help you? What's the matter?" Benny asked timidly.

"Tell your father I want to see him as soon as he gets home!" With that he stomped down the stairs.

Benny and Shirley were as quiet as mice waiting for the cat to pounce.

Mama and Daddy came straight home from the nearby movie theater. The neighbor watched out the window and went out in the hall to greet them. As they approached the landing he jumped out at them.

"Where do you think you live, in a barn? What kind of animals are you raising? Come in here and look what they did!"

They walked into the living room; and smashed on the floor was a large chandelier, wires torn, glass shards scattered everywhere.

"This cost me $200.00. You have to replace it. You better move too because if I ever get my hands on those animals of yours – G-d knows what I might do to them."

Mama and Daddy apologized profusely and promised to pay him.

They walked into our quiet apartment. Benny and Shirley who had also watched for Mama and Daddy through the window sat on the sofa and waited.

"One time we leave you alone and this is how you behave; you can't not fight for a few hours? What is wrong with you?" Daddy bellowed.

"It was an accident. What happened down there?" Shirley sobbed.

"The chandelier fell down; it could have killed someone. Stay away from those people – Mr. Schultz wants to kill you and I don't blame him," Mama yelled.

Benny and Shirley knew they were wrong. Each explained his and her side of the story. They promised that something like that would never happen again.

To my knowledge there were no more big bangs, just the occasional sound of Tiger jumping from the top of the refrigerator, a chest of drawers or a bookcase onto the floor. Tiger was our kitten. We always had a cat; probably a holdover from the farm.

Another of my recollections is of Tiger's bath the day Shirley decided he needed one.

"Tiger is dirty, you can help me give him a bath," she said to me out of the blue.

I was thrilled. She ran the tub and tried to put him into the water. He squirmed and scratched fighting for his life. Before we could clean him he jumped out of the tub, dashed out of the room and hid under a bed.

Now it was time for my part of the job. I lied down on the floor and pleaded,

"Please tiger, come out; psss, psss, psss, here kitty," nothing worked.

When he decided he was ready, he crawled out and ran. Before long he was sneezing. His head down, shoulders slouched he made his way into the living room. We panicked. We thought he was about to die. Shirley had a friend who lived on the top floor whose mother was a nurse. Desperate, we went up and told them the story.

Mrs. Tracy ran down to look at the cat. By this time Tiger was lethargic and he allowed her to examine him. "His nose is warm. He may have a little fever. It looks like he caught a chill and may have a cold. Cats are very resilient though. Try to keep him warm and make sure he has a bowl of water to drink at all times. And, don't let him out – at least until he's better. Whatever you do, no more baths; cats hate water. I think he will be OK in a day or two." she assured us.

Relieved, we managed to cover him with towels and a doll blanket in my doll carriage; no matter how we tried to keep him there he kept jumping out. When we woke up the next morning, we were pleasantly surprised to find him almost completely recovered.

I've always believed that Tiger used the first of his nine lives that evening.

Like the universe, Tiger and I continued to grow and make more memories.

Soon after my "big bang," together we did a bang-up job of improving the family's lifestyle.

Chapter II
Tiny Tiger Triggers Epic Turn

In late December 1943, on one of our regular Sunday visits to the park, Daddy and I walked home, our backs hunched against a cold wind, hands tucked into the pockets of our long winter coats.

Every Sunday morning, no matter the season, Daddy took me to the park. We explored the natural refuge in the midst of the bricks and mortar that made up our neighborhood. Daddy fed stale bred to the squirrels and other critters as we watched them scamper in the brush. It wasn't unusual for a squirrel to climb up on his shoulders as Daddy sat on a bench. Other visitors chastised him:

"Mister, don't you know that they're probably rabid? A bite could kill you!"

Dad just smiled, "why would they bite me when I'm feeding them?"

After spending a few hours, we headed home, taking our usual route along 180th Street. This time, however, as we passed the real estate office, my eye fixed on a dollhouse in the window. I tugged at Daddy's sleeve and pointed.

"Can we buy that house for "Tiger"?

"No," he grinned, "No, that is not a house for Tiger."

"Please, he needs his own house; it's big enough for him, please, please, please! We stood in front of the store debating for some time. Finally, the broker came out.

"Can I help you?"

"No, I don't think so," Daddy responded smiling. "She wants the house in the window for our cat."

"Oh," the man laughed. "No sweetie, that house is only for show; not even your kitten can live in it."

Turning to Daddy he then said:

"But I do have the perfect home for you and your family just a few blocks from here."

Now it was Dad's turn to laugh.

"Thank you, but we're in no position to buy a house."

The broker pressed:

"I promise you will be able to afford this one. Just go look at it" he said writing down the address.

Daddy took the piece of paper and proceeded toward home.

"Daddy why can't we look at the house," I pestered him.

"OK," he agreed after a few minutes; he bypassed our cross street and walked to Daly Avenue. We turned left and walked another four blocks to 1972, the sixth of a row of seven detached small private houses that occupied one half of the northeast side of the street. It was a tiny, gray wood frame house with white trim and shutters; green and white striped awnings kept the sun at bay. Daddy's eyes lit up. He was very unhappy living in a cramped apartment.

"Everyone should own a piece of property. People should not have to live on top of each other in chicken coops," was one of his many mantras about the human condition.

As soon as we walked in the door of our apartment, I excitedly blurted the whole story to Mama, finishing with:

"Can we please buy the house?"

"What is she talking about? We have no money to buy a house," she replied looking at Daddy in disbelief.

"I know," he conceded, "but it's an estate sale and the broker says it's priced to sell. It looks to be in excellent condition. How much do we have in the bank?"

"A few dollars and we need it to live on. We can't afford a house!" she scowled.

I pleaded: "please mommy, please, just come look at it."

"It won't hurt to look at it," Daddy reluctantly urged. Finally she agreed just to appease us.

When she set eyes on the minuscule colonial with its white fence she couldn't help but smile. She wanted nothing more than to be able to move out of the small apartment her family of five shared after having enjoyed ten years on the farm especially after Shirley and Benny played havoc with the neighbor's nerves.

Still thinking it was impossible for them to buy it, Mom and Dad summoned the courage to look into the matter a bit further and scheduled an inspection. When they saw the interior, the back porch and the little garden, all in pristine condition, they were hooked. Mama fell in love with the five-piece cherry mahogany salon set — a love seat, two large and two smaller chairs, all with curved arms and majestic straight, carved backs with tufted, gold velvet upholstery. In the adjoining 9' x 12' dining room, she admired a set of oak furniture, complete with a round claw-footed table and four high backed burgundy velvet chairs, a curved glass china closet, a buffet, and a "Morrison" recliner.

It turned out that the $800.00 Mama had managed to save for living during the off-season was just enough for the down payment, moving and move-in expenses. With low taxes and a $3,000.00 privately held, interest-only mortgage Mom and Dad decided they could buy the house after all. The heirs to the estate had no interest in it or its contents and threw in the furniture for an additional $25.00.

So it was that a routine trip to the park, a small child, a cat and a doll house brought together a home and a family in need. That house saw us through trying times; bore witness to the intricacies and intimacies of growing up, growing old, and passing on, along with untold adventures, misadventures and strange encounters for more than twenty-six years.

Part II
Daly Avenue, The Bronx Circa 1940s and 1950s

Chapter 12
New Residents Revive Old Residence

A musty smell, layers of dust and a strange eeriness greeted us as we entered the house after the closing. I tagged along with Mama and Daddy as they carefully looked at everything for the first time.

"They died here, one-by-one, two brothers and a sister," Daddy whispered to Mama."

"Don't remind me," she replied, wincing. "It's been empty for the last few years. We're going to have a lot of work to do around here."

As we made our way down the squeaky steps to the basement, I thought for sure I heard the ghosts of the previous owners walking below.

What we found instead were old pipes, tools, newspapers, stacks of books and bric-a-brac neatly stored along with more than twenty bird cages; neighbors said that one of the brothers restored them for resale. Besides the furniture in the living room and dining room that was thrown into the purchase price for an additional $25.00, the three bedrooms upstairs were also fully furnished. Mom and Dad carefully examined each piece.

"We can use this dresser; look at the wood frame on that mirror," said Mama.

"OK, how about this chest of drawers" Daddy countered.

In the end, they kept two dressers with mirrors along with the chest and a few miscellaneous pieces. They discarded old beds, magazines and sundry unwanted items and used the proceeds from sales of the bird cages, lamps and bric-a-brac to more than cover the cost of a new bedroom set and two twin beds, window shades, curtains and other accoutrements.

Since the house had been empty for so long, they also made up their minds to paint the entire interior before taking up residence. Conveniently, one of our new neighbors, Mr. Tag ran a painting business out of the big white stucco house on the corner where he lived with his wife and a caretaker.

Mr. Tag assigned Tony to the job. An artist by profession, he worked as a house painter to stave off the "starving artist" syndrome. Thirteen year-old pubescent Shirley instantly became obsessed with Tony's seductive brown eyes, thick dark hair and perceptive smile. Every afternoon she dragged me to the house to monitor Tony's artistic "advances" while trying to ply her puerile feminine wiles.

Tony, a native of Italy listened to the radio and sang along with the occasional opera while he took his time to turn every wall in the house into his own personal canvas. Using carefully chosen colors, stencils and decorative techniques, he bestowed on each room, including the hallways and bathroom, its own character.

The kitchen was the pièce de résistance. He spent days in this one 9' x 12' room, masterfully entwining veins of green, black, white and gray paint on the lower four feet of the walls, crowning his granite-like masterpiece with a high gloss black border and topping it off with white walls and ceiling.

No cabinets, appliances or furniture would eclipse the distinctive mural; a small white porcelain sink stood in the corner next to the window and, in the diagonally opposite corner, a built-in white china closet with three drawers in its base and four cabinets above with glass paneled doors receded into the landscape.

The room had never actually been used as a kitchen. Rather, it served as the passageway to the bona fide kitchen in the basement. That was where the family gathered around the potbelly stove to stay warm; where Mom prepared meals on a gas stove with its upright oven that was used not only for baking and broiling, but for making toast as well. A metal kitchen table with matching chairs rounded out the eating area.

A black double slop-sink stood in one back corner; the door to the backyard in the other. A small vestibule in the front of the house was home to an ice box that left barely enough room to open the doors. The boiler room contained a coal furnace, a suspended twenty-gallon water tank and a miniscule hot water boiler.

The coal bin was in the other front corner. The precious resource was delivered via a window chute, while adjustable wood planks held the coal inside when the door was opened to retrieve coal. The bin held nine tons of coal but was rarely filled to capacity. More often, we bought it one or two tons at a time.

Wood crates from neighborhood stores, ideal for kindling, often made up for the coal we couldn't afford. Mom made deals with the people hired by produce and other store owners to discard empty crates, to drop them off in our front yard.

Sometimes, Dad got his hands on some logs that burned a lot slower and he chopped them on a tree stump, turned chopping block, outside the back basement door. When he was lucky enough to find a tree trunk, he put it on wooden horse and together, he and I sawed it with a two-person saw.

More often than not, however, it was Mom who used the chopping block.

After a while with each swing of the axe, her hands dirty and nose smudged with dirt, she cursed the privation that led to this task.

She kept the house relatively warm but only managed hot water when absolutely needed for weekend baths (no shower), weekly house-cleaning, laundry and dishwashing. On many days, dirty dishes stayed stacked in the sink waiting for hot water. Other household chores waited too.

As I got older, I was in a perpetual state of embarrassment about the house, the wood boxes in front yard and my clothes often in need of laundering.

Despite my humiliation, a constant stream of visitors of all ages felt at home in what came to be known by many as "Beck's farm."

Chapter 13
Welcoming Committee of One

"Hi, I'm Lenny, we're the supers of that building," he gestured toward the corner building across the street.

"I'm Susie, we just moved in," I replied barely audibly.

"I'm a big super and you're a little one" he continued.

Despite the disparity in our positions, we went on to become best friends and so did our mothers. Lenny, four days younger than I, took me on a tour of his building and showed me the big boiler, coal bins and how they collected garbage from the dumbwaiters.

We played together and spent lots of time in each other's homes. Mostly we played doctor where he was the doctor and I the patient. He didn't want to play house, a girls game, but we somehow kissed quite a bit; that is until we started school. After I dropped out of kindergarten and left the school we attended together, he quickly became enamored by another girl. Word got back to me:

"Lenny likes Libby now," Rita instigated.

Upset, I whined to Mama and Mrs. Eifler:

"After I wasted all that spit on him, now he likes Libby."

They looked at each other and couldn't help but laugh; they often reminded me of that line.

An unlikely pair, they were inseparable. Mrs. Eifler stopped at our house every day. The two talked, laughed and helped each other through tough times.

A short time after we moved onto the block, Mr. Eifler, a longshoreman with a severe drinking problem failed to return home from work. Several weeks passed before he was found floating in the waters off Brooklyn. Mrs. Eifler began cleaning houses to supplement her small superintendent income. Her older son Michael was in his early teens. One of her employers, who was in the construction business, gave Michael a job to help his Mom. He soon developed into quite a hunk from time spent outdoors and heavy lifting; my friends and I took note.

Upon her arrival from Romania, Mrs. Eifler had worked as a servant for a rich family where she learned to cook and bake. Often when I played with Lenny, she prepared what she called "rich" potatoes just like the ones she made for her rich employers; she removed the meat of a baked potato — mashed it with butter, milk and salt — put it back in the shell, and back into the oven to brown. Come Christmas time, she made the greatest cookies; her egg-white kisses, butter cookies and linzer tarts melted in your mouth.

In our teens, as is often the case, Lenny and I drifted apart. We each had different friends and lost touch even though we continued to live on the same block. He, like his brother, worked at a very young age. At about 6'5" tall by the time he was thirteen he was an imposing force and soon became a star usher at RKO theaters throughout the borough.

I was pleasantly surprised one day in 2003 when I received an e-mail from an old classmate with a copy of an article Lenny had written that appeared in a publication called "Back to The Bronx." It activated each and every one of my senses: the sounds of trolleys, coal deliveries, Bungalow Bar and Good Humor ice cream truck melodies, and the strolling violinist who serenaded the tenement dwellers for a few coins wrapped in paper and thrown from windows. I virtually tasted the vanilla melleroles, kosher hot dogs, and pizza he recalled.

He talked about our Saturdays at the movies. He didn't mention that we used to be called on stage at the Vogue theater on the Saturday afternoon closest to our birthdays; or that on one such occasion when we were ten, because of his extraordinary height they presented him with a baby bottle filled with ice cream from which he good naturedly tried in vain to extract the delicacy through the nipple.

Lenny went on to Stuyvesant High School in Manhattan which was a high performing school that required passing an entrance exam. He married young and started a family. His first marriage ended in divorce. In the end he remarried and settled with his family to Orlando, Florida.

His brother had enlisted in the Air Force, married and raised a family in San Antonio, Texas as a career officer.

The friendship between Mama and Katie Eifler continued until Mama's death and beyond. When in her later years, Katie was all alone in the Bronx, Arnie and I helped her in any way we could with frequent phone calls, visits to our home, shopping and driving.

In her seventies, she declined efforts by her sons to relocate to Florida or Texas. She still maintained a few of her early housecleaning clients and dragged her declining body, disfigured by Osteoporosis, from the Bronx to Queens by a network of busses.

One evening in the mid-1980s I received a call from her neighbor telling me that Katie had fallen while shopping in a local store and was hospitalized. I immediately called her and she sounded OK. I told her I would see her the next day. Instead I received a second call the next morning to say that she had passed during the night.

I felt like I lost another mother and wondered if Mama would now be a welcoming committee of one for her dear friend.

Chapter 14
Humble Estate

Lenny was right about the size of our respective domains; his was big and mine little. Mama called it our dollhouse, an accurate analogy. The property was all of 25 x 40 feet; one third allocated to a back porch (in modern parlance – a deck) and garden. The footprint of the two story dwelling measured 20' x 25' for a grand total of approximately 1,000 square feet of living space – plus an additional 200 square foot basement.

This was huge to us, coming from a 500 square foot apartment. It made a significant difference in our lifestyle and comfort. The architects had made efficient use of the limited area with small but functional rooms and a layout that afforded everyone their own space – even if at times it was comparable to a closet. Many interior design touches also added a distinctive elegance usually reserved for larger more affluent homes.

First, one entered a 3' x 3' vestibule with an interior door, a feature I have not been able to duplicate in any future homes. Upon entering the foyer to the left, one was welcomed by a stairway to heaven visible through a stained glass skylight. The dark mahogany banister was supported by white turned balusters. Atop the lower post a bronze colored sculpture of a statuesque woman on tip toe, skirt askew, holding a torch lit the way. At the top of the steps, a simple sconce, with a glass shade that matched the torch, worked in concert with it.

The living room was off the foyer to the right. Twin windows faced the street. The mahogany and velvet loveseat was the focal point in the center of the facing wall. Two large matching chairs flanked it in each of the far corners, and two smaller chairs filled the two remaining corners. A round marble-topped coffee table in front of the couch, under a five light chandelier that hung on a chain from a cherub decorated disc in the middle of the ceiling completed the room.

A second door led to the adjoining dining room that faced the back of the house. The round oak table and four burgundy velvet upholstered chairs stood in the center. A large buffet with a full-width, wood framed mirror occupied one full wall. A curved glass, carved china closet stood in one corner and a mission style manual recliner in another.

This room also opened into the kitchen. In addition to the doorway from the dining room, the kitchen had egress to the back porch, the foyer and the basement. The inordinate number of doors limited space and utility. That was probably one reason the former owners used the basement as their kitchen; we did too until many years later.

Upstairs, the first and very important room at the top of the steps was the single bathroom – with its claw-footed tub, small hand sink and toilet – no shower. At the opposite end of the foyer, the master bedroom faced the front of the house. A second bedroom faced the rear; the third, so-called bedroom could only be accessed from the master bedroom. At 8' x 10' it resembled a walk-in closet more than a bedroom.

Mom, Dad and I shared the master bedroom. The back room was Benny's and Shirley drew the short straw and ended up with the "little room."

Compact as it was, for us the dollhouse was the real thing . . . a home at last.

Chapter 15
Streetscape

Like many blocks in the city, our street had apartment buildings with stores on street level. Add the wide variety of retailers just around the corner on Tremont Avenue and we lived in the midst of a three-block, self-contained mini-metropolis.

Tremont Avenue is a main east/west thoroughfare. It was a vibrant, bustling shopping area. The southwest corner was home to "Meister's House Wares" where you could pick up anything from a sewing thimble or can opener to a complete set of towels or curtains fit for the finest home. Down the street, three sole proprietors practiced their crafts at Sam's Barber Shop, Charlie's Chinese Laundry and Tony's Shoe Repair.

On our side of the street, "Goretsky's Pharmacy" occupied the corner store. Then there was the candy store with revolving ownership, "Phil's Bikes" rental and repair and a cleaning store. A fourth store was rented to a variety of transient tenants including a family of gypsies; Mama was sure that one day they would kidnap me. She warned:

"Don't go near them. In Europe they took small children and nobody ever saw them again."

All of these establishments played major roles in my growing up. The candy store was my second home especially when Mrs. Hanlin owned it. She was a single mother with a daughter Doris who was may age and my friend. So, you can imagine my shock when Shirley came in from the candy store, chomping on a giant piece of bubble gum.

"I want that," I said immediately.

"Too bad, you can't have it. Mrs. Hanlin is only selling it to her best customers."

"And Susie's not a good customer, Mama questioned. "What do you mean?

"She just got a small amount in so she's saving them for her best customers."

It turned out that Fleer's Double Bubble gum was rationed because something in it was used for military purposes until 1942. After that it was slowly reintroduced and was in short supply. Of course Mama went right next door to the candy store and got me a square inch cube of my own. I can still taste the victory.

Later, it was in that same candy store that I first heard "Rock around the Clock" playing in the juke box. About that time I also became an unpaid soda jerk: I served fountain favorites like "a two-cents plain,' cherry coke, and of course, the New York special – foamy chocolate egg creams. Not too long after that I bought loose cigarettes for two-cents each; a pack cost 18 cents.

Next door at Phil's I rented bikes and I learned to ride a two-wheeler a half-hour at a time; cost: thirty minutes for a quarter. I can't count the number of times Mr. Goretsky (pharmacists often administered first aid in those days) tended a badly scraped knee, took something out of my eye and especially when he bandaged a severe gash in my skull. The permanent dent is a constant reminder of Eugene accidentally landing on my head when he jumped from a ledge to the front entrance of the basement where I was standing.

First aid was just one of many services available right around the corner. On Tremont Avenue there was a store for every need; a dairy, a butcher, a fish store, fresh produce, deli, fast food and best of all a bakery from which aromas of sugar cookies, fresh baked rye bread and onion rolls, not to mention delicious cakes, drifted through our open windows.

The neighborhood was characteristic of working-class communities throughout the boroughs. Many families were made up of immigrant parents and their first generation American offspring. Most earned their livings at blue-collar jobs and mothers stayed home to take care of us.

Few owned cars. Most couldn't afford them, nor did they need them. Schools, shopping, movie theaters and nearly all services were within walking distance. Dependable public transportation was readily available as well. The Lexington and Seventh Avenue trains stopped at the elevated station a few blocks away at West Farms Square. Trolleys, and later buses, ran on Tremont Avenue and nearby East 180th Street.

Our neighborhood, like most in the boroughs, was a multinational, self sufficient community in the mosaic that is New York City.

Chapter 16
Living Standards Rise as Enemies Fall

Many Americans feared that the end of World War II and the subsequent drop in military spending might bring back the hard times of the "Great Depression." Instead, pent-up consumer demand fueled economic growth. Businesses turned war production back to consumer markets. New industries sprang up and returning veterans furthered their educations.

The fortunes of most of the working-class began to rise. Unfortunately we remained behind the curve. Dad's seasonal work still barely provided enough to live on.

Theoretically, owning a private house was an indication of at least low middle-income status. For us, nothing could have been further from the truth. In reality, the house kept us from living on the streets because the tax collector and mortgage holder were more lenient than most landlords would have been, allowing us to postpone tax and mortgage payments. Had we rented we would have surely been evicted by landlords who would have demanded their rent on the first or fifteenth of every month. After a few months of non-payment, tenants were evicted and their furniture and belongings were put on the street.

The coal supplier, on the other hand, wasn't so generous. Many days and nights the house was freezing despite Mama frantically chopping wood crates in a futile attempt to chase away the cold.

While we were the last to acquire the latest new technology like a phone in the house or a TV, Mama always had good relations with local storekeepers so we never went hungry.

The end of war drove the standard of living for the working class higher but we did not go along for the ride.

Chapter 17
Shangri-La in the City

Regardless of our economic status, outside our home, the casual passerby might hear the murmur of a radio, children laughing or perhaps loud voices of adults quarrelling. Mama and Daddy frequently clashed over money problems, Benny and Shirley had sibling squabbles, and everyone yelled at me from time to time.

Most likely, one would see large groups of people of all ages sitting on and around the small stoop talking, playing checkers, or watching a game of box ball or hit the penny. One thing he or she would not surmise was what lay behind the small, simple, house set in this urban environment.

In late March, Mom began her elaborate preparations for the colorful, quiet, harmonious rendezvous snugly tucked into this inner-city community. She could be found running around the house with a half dozen egg crates turned propagation trays. She carried them from window sill to window sill, to catch every ray of the rising and setting sun. Her precious cargo contained tiny plantlets that she sowed from seeds that I purchased at school for two-cents per package. They would later be placed in the backyard garden.

It was divided into four segments. The center one measured five-by-twelve feet and was flanked on each end by a four-by-six foot bed. One long narrow bed, approximately eighteen inches wide ran the full width of the property on the far side. Each section was bordered by a single row of mostly red bricks standing on end and an eighteen-inch wide path that wended its way around to link the parts together.

Soon after the April rains subsided, crimson, pink, and yellow tulips along with carrot tipped white daffodils sprang up to announce the beginning of spring. Toward the end of May, when the threat of frost had passed, Mom transplanted the young seedlings from the egg crates into the garden. Dad covered them with his homemade cold frames. The two-foot square, reusable wood frames with sloping sides and glass tops welcomed the warm sun to help stimulate growth and protect the delicate plantlets from excess rain, wind, squirrels, and other predators.

By June, our backyard was a veritable garden of Giverny—a kaleidoscope of purple, alabaster, ginger zinnias, multihued asters, and deep orange and golden marigolds joined together as if by the hand of Monet. Half a dozen perennial rose bushes delighted the senses with a wide assortment of sizes, colors, and fragrances. The rose of Sharon in the middle of the long flower bed awoke, and soon scores of deep pink flora opened and flourished well into fall.

Some summers, violet and white morning glories wove their way through the somewhat rusty chain link fence that separated our property from the adjacent backyard of the firehouse around the corner. Other years, green beans climbed the wire squares, monitoring the growing progress of tomatoes, peppers, or cucumbers.

Most mornings Mom was out early, working her own special organic fertilizer —leftover egg whites and shells, coffee grinds, along with remains of the previous night's dinner – into the soil. She sprinkled tobacco, scavenged from ashtrays full of Daddy's cigarette butts, to keep creepy-crawly critters away. Finally, she weeded, pruned, and preened as needed.

An 8' x 12' foot porch overlooked the garden. After it was rebuilt following a fire in 1948, which destroyed the entire back of the house, Shirley painstakingly painted it to match the newly repainted exterior of the house. She coated the floor with a matching buttery cream color, carefully added a green border, and finished it with a fleur-de-lis design in the center and four corners. For the hand rails and banisters leading to the garden, she laid forest green atop the one-inch cream-colored balusters. Finally, she carried the color scheme to the set of Adirondack furniture that Dad had built. A love seat, two chairs and a twenty-four-inch round, pedestal table that opened for storage greeted friends and neighbors.

Whether I was playing house with my girlfriends, maintaining my balance as I walked on the garden bricks heel-to-toe, or digging my way to China; if Benny or Shirley were hanging out with their friends; or Mom and Dad chatted on the porch with neighbors, this secluded hideaway was a multi-generational escape.

Nurtured by a mutual love of nature shared by Mama and Daddy, Daddy's carpentry skills, Shirley's artistic flair and Mama's tender gardening, this Shangri-la provided a welcome diversion from untold hardship, conflict, and angst that all too often pervaded the humble home that hid them from view.

Chapter 18
Next Door Neighbors

Community played a big role in our lives. Unlike today when we rarely know our neighbors, in the forties they were extended family. Ours came from a multiplicity of ethnic backgrounds — Jewish, German, Irish, Italian, and a variety of other combinations. Some were immigrants, others first generation Americans, families who called America home for many generations, and one Native American, Dickie Fairchild, a friend of Benny and Shirley. They spoke in a cacophony of brogues, accents and dialects.

Helen and Joe Fiskey lived next door with three grown children, Josie, Michael and Jimmy. Joe was a second generation Italian; Helen was born in Cuba and never learned English. With her Yiddish accent, Mama frequently chatted with Helen over the fence. It was obvious and amusing that each understood little of what the other said. Their conversations, however, seemed to be animated and satisfying. Perhaps complete comprehension is not a necessary component of a good sounding board that often helps deal with anxieties.

One day Mama's friend, Mrs. Jakel, was visiting. She listened to them, a quizzical look on her face, and asked Mama in Yiddish:

"Vos hut ze gezukt (what did she say?)," to which Mom replied:

"Ver Vaist (Who knows?)," to which Helen smiled amicably.

Despite their language and cultural differences, the two Helens would do anything for each other. It was in their basement that I awoke on that fateful morning when our house caught fire. Awakened by the fire engines, the Fiskeys immediately invited us into their basement, a large room where they ate, slept, and spent most of their time. Helen brewed strong Cuban coffee that she served with lots of milk in white round ceramic bowls.

As soon as the bakery around the corner opened Joe went and bought fresh Kaiser rolls. They slathered them with fresh tub butter purchased from the small family grocery store and turned a near catastrophe into a warm get-together (no pun intended). I was only nine, but when I woke up — startled, not understanding what I was doing there — I too was given a bowl of coffee, albeit heavier on the milk, along with a scrumptious cholesterol laden roll.

Joe and Helen were among the few on the block who had a car. We traveled with them often. She loaded the car with baskets of cooked corn on the cob, sandwiches, drinks, and fresh fruit. We piled into the 1946 Oldsmobile and went to Jones Beach or Ronkonkoma to visit Helen's sister. There were no major highways yet so we often rode two-to-three hours in each direction. When we felt hunger pangs, Joe pulled to the side of the road, opened folding chairs and food baskets that were in the trunk, and we picnicked right there. Every once and a while a car passed and the passengers waved.

One Sunday morning, on the spur of the moment, we set out to visit Benny at school. After the long ride to Doylestown, we encountered a virtually empty campus. We walked around looking for a person, any person. We wandered into several empty dorms. Finally we came upon a barn where a student tended cows. We asked if he knew Benny Beck. He didn't. Shirley asked, "do you know Boom Boom?" using his nickname. The young man deliberated for a moment and shaking his head pensively responded:

"No, I'm sorry; I don't know the names of the cows."

Amused but disappointed, we headed back toward home. About a mile from the school we saw two young men hitchhiking. As we caught up we recognized an unmistakable familial walk. They turned out to be Benny and a buddy. Our surprise was exceeded only by Benny's wide-eyed speechlessness when he looked into the car and saw all of us. There was no more room in the car so the two boys jumped on the running board and we drove back to the school.

In their senior years, the Fiskeys moved to Jacksonville, Florida. Joe soon fell in love with a younger, American-born woman and left Helen after some forty years of marriage. He drove her back to New York to stay with her sister on Long Island. But first they stopped at our house for a few days.

During that very difficult time the two Helens, who had spent so much time talking across the fence, commiserated night after night. Language was still not an issue. Now, however, they communicated primarily with tears as Mama tried desperately to console her neighbor who had long ago become a good friend.

Chapter 19
Coming to My Senses

Metal trolley car wheels screeched against tracks that wound their way along the full length of Tremont Avenue. Fire bells rang and sirens screamed at all hours of the day and night. Firehouse Company 45 was just around the corner; their yard backed up on ours. They were such great neighbors; after a short time we didn't even hear the noise — just enjoyed watching them play basketball in the backyard while they waited for an alarm to sound.

Peddlers' shouts announced their produce specials of the day:

"Get your fresh corn, ripe tomatoes; juicy watermelon."

Horses that pulled the wagons stirred our olfactory senses as they littered the streets on which we played. Little Eugene, so named because Big Eugene was taller, picked up the dung on a stick, flung it at passers by and fled, laughing hysterically. I recently heard that he retired at age forty-five after making a killing on Wall Street.

We waited in anticipation for the bell that signaled the daily arrival of the small cottage shaped truck that carried Bungalow Bar, the best ice cream in town. A clapper sounded the coming of the coconut man, who sold cut up coconut by the slice, and the knife sharpener who appeared periodically to finely hone the edges on knives, scissors, and tools like saws, chisels, and axes.

Grilling onions, hamburgers, hot dogs, and French fries with mustard, not ketchup, summoned us to the open window of the "Busy Bee Restaurant."

Walking on the Avenue was a common pastime. The Nose always knew precisely where we were. Fresh bread, cookies, and chocolate cake beckoned from the bakery.

The scent of sour pickles signified we were passing "Daitch's" supermarket where we picked a pickle for a nickel out of a barrel. Preserved in vinegar and brine, it packed an amalgam of all our senses in each bite; it crunched, dripped, smelled and made our lips pucker. Kosher corned beef and pastrami wafted from "Heimy's" delicatessen, and if you sniffed tomato sauce and cheese you had to be passing the "Pines" restaurant.

The store next door sold only one product, the Charlotte Russe. This confection consisted of a small piece of vanilla cake in a white cardboard half-cup, topped with a four-inch high tower of fresh whipped cream that swirled out of a big shiny silver machine and was crowned with a bright red cherry. Beside this delectable treat and other epicurean delights, we had plenty of eye candy.

Saturday movies were an all day adventure, featuring two full length films, a dozen cartoons, coming attractions (now known as trailers, which seems to be a misnomer) and the newsreel of the week, all for a quarter. Some theaters gave out flyers advertising upcoming events, and a coupon for a free ice cream cone nearby. Moreover, movie theaters were one of few venues that were air conditioned, offering an added bonus during hot summer months.

On Thursday evenings our mothers went for dishes, given away, one to a customer. We accumulated a whole set of "Vogue Theater" dishes including a serving platter, sugar bowl and creamer. And, Tuesday was "amateur night" at the movies when wannabe entertainers had the opportunity to juggle, tell jokes and sing for our listening pleasure.

Our tactile senses were activated by the streets as we crawled all over the middle of tarred intersections to flick soda bottle caps filled with banana peel through a series of numbered boxes in a chalk-drawn game called Skulley. The object was to stay out of the skull, a box drawn in the center. If you landed there you could not move and therefore lost your ability to kill off opponents. The winner was the last player standing. We often played multiple games at a time, each taking about a half hour depending on the number of players; only an occasional passing car interrupted this and other street games like "kick the can," "off the curb" and stickball, the most popular game where the entire street was the playing field.

My sixth sense tells me that although we did not benefit from today's high tech toys, games and the incredible internet, our need to use our imaginations, creativity and competitive natures helped shape a strong, hard-working post-war generation that contributed in a big way to the growth of the country.

Chapter 20
Rhode Island Reds Roost Here

Cock-a-doodle-do, cock-a-doodle-do — a natural wake-up call in much of the nation's heartland perhaps — but in the Bronx?

"What the hell is that? It's four o'clock in the morning." Joe yelled.

"Oh that must be the Becks' rooster; they got some chickens," said Helen.

Soon after we moved into the house Daddy seemed to think he was back on the farm. For the last several years of apartment living he had been craving fresh eggs. Finally he got his wish. His aha moment came when he spied some squandered space under the back porch. By the summer of 1946 he had removed stored wood, crates and debris from the opening and enclosed it with wire mesh nailed to a series of 2 x 4's to create a chicken coop. He hinged one of the 4-foot panels to open and close for easy access. Next he bought some nesting boxes, feeding dishes, several perches and wood chips to spread all over the ground. Once completed, Dad stocked the coop with eight live hens, a rooster, and plenty of feed.

At seven, I was overjoyed. We always had cats and even a puppy that unfortunately died of Distemper after just a few weeks. But to get a whole flock of pets in one fell swoop was overwhelming. I loved my new chickens with their funny looking orange crowns; I watched them roam around and peck at the ground to hunt for food as they cackled, clucked and chirped. The rooster wasn't too friendly. He marched around the yard like a sentinel guarding his hens; his black feathers, red earlobes, wattles and crest confirmed his bad-guy image.

Several months after the feathered family settled in, Dad came out one morning to find the first eggs. His taste buds would once more delight in newly picked eggs with plump, deep orange yolks. He brought six in and cracked one open.

"Now that's a fresh egg; look at that color," he said, grinning.

He dropped a big chunk of butter in a pan, cracked another egg and placed the two big, firm, fresh eggs in the sizzling skillet; he savored the flavor along with buttered toast and a cup of hot percolated coffee.

Mom fried a batch sunny side up. The perfectly round sunbursts transported the family back in time. Since I was merely an embryo when they were enjoying the fruits of the farm, I was not similarly affected. Besides I wouldn't eat an egg unless it was completely fried and drowned in ketchup.

Each morning Mama went out to gather the newly laid eggs for breakfast and to give to neighbors. One day in early fall a gentlemen rang the bell, introduced himself as an investigator from the Board of Health and showed his credentials. He looked around and appeared a bit perplexed at the incongruity of what he was about to say.

"We received a complaint about chickens making noise. Do you have chickens here?"

Mom took him out back and showed him the suspects. It turned out that the neighborhood troublemaker had called the authorities. She had alleged that a rooster was disturbing her peace, waking her in the wee hours of the morning. The inspector went on to explain:

"According to statute, to be valid, the complainant must live within fifty feet of the offensive noise. I see here that the complainant lives five houses away from you so you can keep your chickens if there are no other complaints."

Mom and Dad, however, decided to dispose of the chickens in the interest of maintaining the good-neighbor policy and to avoid further problems with the complainant.

There was no ready market for pet chickens, which meant that my feathered friends had to go to the slaughterhouse. To conform to Jewish dietary laws, they had to undergo ritual slaughter by a Shochet - Hebrew for a butcher who is well versed in Jewish kosher law. The method of slaughter is a quick, deep cut across the throat that instantly renders the animal unconscious. It is thought to be painless; in fact it is widely recognized as being humane. It also ensures rapid and complete draining of the blood, another requirement of kosher law.

Every Friday for as many weeks as there were chickens, Mom trapped one in a cage and carried it to the closest kosher live poultry market in the Morris Park section of the Bronx. We didn't own a car and public transportation was not an option with a live chicken in tow, so she walked the mile from home. Sometimes I accompanied her.

The chicken market was in a big warehouse. Men, most bearded, with blood under their fingernails and all over their white coats walked among lots of chickens, waddling about, oblivious to their forthcoming fate. Buying fresh chickens from live markets was not uncommon at the time, but we were probably the only customers to bring our own.

One evening, at dinner, it hit me.

"Is this the chicken we brought to the market today?" I screamed.

My sick feeling was confirmed by a series of conspiratorial glances between Mama, Daddy, Benny and Shirley.

I burst into hysterics, gagged as my stomach turned into a violently erupting volcano.

I never went back to the fresh market, nor did poultry pass my lips for many years hence.

Chapter 21
Characters Welcome

Mama had an open door policy. Folks came and went at will. Neighbors, laden down with bundles from their daily shopping stopped in to chat and rest before climbing the steps to their apartments. Mrs. Gluck and Mrs. Klausz who lived in the corner building came by in the afternoons. On many a pleasant spring or fall evening Mr. Klausz or Mr. Gluck joined their wives on the stoop along with the Gluck's dog, duke.

A host of odd, lonely eccentrics also found their way to our humble home. Mrs. Abramowitz, an always well groomed divorcee in her mid to late sixties visited daily. Dad had come out one morning and found her in front of the house, dizzy, sweaty and feeling faint.

"Are you ok?" he asked.

"No, I think I'm going to pass out," she responded. "Can I have a little water?"

He brought the water and offered her a chair. From that moment on she became a regular. It was her habit to constantly sniff herself, convinced that her ex-husband spitefully put feces on her clothing, shoes and handbags.

Mrs. Hagopa, a wild-eyed woman, in her early fifties had lived next door to us before we moved to the house. Paranoid beyond belief, her eyes darted all around monitoring the area for "them." She lined her walls with aluminum foil to keep out the malevolent rays of illusory evil doers who were out to get her.

"They listen to everything and watch me all the time," she'd say.

Then there was Mr. Cohen always meticulously attired in a perfectly pressed suit, shirt and tie. A bachelor in his sixties as well, he knew father from the furrier's union; he simply had no one to talk to at home so he often stayed well into the night.

"What am I going to do, talk to the four walls." he lamented.

Miss Reiter, a "Seventh-Day Adventist," came by one day as part of a neighborhood canvas to recruit members. Daddy made the mistake of listening and disputing some of the tenets she espoused. As a highly trained salesperson, his action brought her back regularly to try to answer his objections.

He mischievously sparred with her about biblical interpretations which only encouraged her to work harder.

"It's right here," she would say, reading from a passage from the Holy Scriptures:

" 'Join us and you will be part of the new earth. On the new earth, in which righteousness dwells, God will provide an eternal home for the redeemed and a perfect environment for everlasting life, love, joy, and learning in His presence.' You see, there is life after death."

"I'm not arguing 'life after death,'" Dad responded, "sure life goes on after we die, but unfortunately not for the deceased; it goes on through our children and the people whose lives we touch on our journey."

The weekly verbal jousting went on for many years.

Mr. Segal was a kibitzer who lived on the next block. He stopped in often on his way home from the Avenue. His famous opening line was:

"Hello, I haven't spoken to you in a long distance, what's new?"

His claim to fame was that he had never brushed his teeth or seen a dentist, yet he still had every one of his original teeth at seventy-seven. He also told stories about his experiences in the Russian Army during World War I.

Mrs. Scharfman lived five houses away from us in a two-family house. She was the neighborhood trouble maker and the one responsible for the demise of our chickens. A frequent visitor when we first moved in, she quickly wore out her welcome. She fought with every neighbor – accusing kids and adults alike of giving her dirty looks, disturbing her dogs or somehow interfering with her landlady/tenant relations. The last straw for Mama was when she complained to the Department of Housing about our fine feathered friends.

After he moved away from home, her husband, Mr. Scharfman used to come by periodically to check on his grown sons. He would look both ways to ensure that no one saw him and ring our bell. Despite his caution and the infrequency of his inquiries his wife caught him talking to Mama one day at our front door. He saw her and ran for his life.

"You whore" she yelled at Mama, "you're having an affair with my husband. He left me for you, you tramp, you!"

Mama quickly closed the door and retreated to the back of the house. Given the constant flow of traffic it would have been impossible to engage in a romantic relationship even if she was so inclined. And, if she were of a mind to do so, it would surely not be with Mr. Scharfman.

Mrs. Schwartz owned the two-family house next door to Mrs. Scharfman. She came constantly to grumble about her tenants, the Lynch's; they had the audacity to demand heat in the winter.

"God bless the radiators in that house," she said "they are warm *even* when I don't put the heat up." In the meantime Shirley's good friend was Betty Lynch. She, her parents and four siblings all wore winter coats indoors as did Mr. and Mrs. Schwartz and their son Marvin. When Shirley and Betty encountered Mrs. Schwartz at our house, they broke into song: "the old gray mare; she ain't what she used to be"

Rose Millstein lived blocks away but began coming to our house to visit with her friend of Mrs. Eifler; she was unable to walk up five flights of stairs to Mrs. Eifler's top floor apartment. Before long, Rose visited us when Mrs. Eifler wasn't there. A bachelorette in her late sixties, she refused to acknowledge her age and insisted that we kids call her by her first name, something we had to get used to. On many a Sunday morning she took Lenny and me to Bickford's cafeteria for English Muffins, their nooks and crannies overflowing with melted butter, and a good strong cup of their signature brew. We were nine and I have still to find better muffins or coffee. Years later Rose went to live in a senior citizen residence but that didn't last.

"They're old people. I don't belong there," she whined before relocating to a SRO (Single Resident Occupancy). There her cohabitants were younger than she. Like most occupants of SRO's, they were unable to maintain long-term relationships or hold steady jobs, and often had drug habits and/or criminal records.

Another of our sojourners was the nice elderly man with a white beard whose job it was to periodically drop off and pick up collection boxes known as "pishkas," to be given to various charities. I learned much later in life that his maturity or philanthropic endeavors did not stop him from trying to also pick up a squeeze of a woman's breast here and there along the way. The list goes on.

Sometimes Shirley, my friends and I played Rummy, Casino or checkers with the old folks. Often we listened in on their tales and later made fun of them. It wasn't always amusing; sometimes arguments broke out and Mama became a referee.

Notwithstanding the humor, and or discord, we, especially Shirley, yearned for privacy. Benny, away at college for most of the time, escaped a good part of all these comings and goings.

It was particularly frustrating to wake up late on a weekend morning, go downstairs in crumpled pajamas, hair disheveled, with only a perfunctory washing of the hands and face, to find one or more of the troupe already sitting at the dining table. After receiving the once-over they watched as each morsel of breakfast entered our mouths. Shirley balked repeatedly:

"What the hell is this, a home or Grand Central Station?"

I still don't understand why these strange visitors were always in our house, why they are indelibly engraved in my memory, or how their perpetual presence and exposure to their eccentricities at such a tender age may have affected who I became.

Part III
Profiles of Primary Players

Chapter 22
Dad

The Dad I knew was an older man as dad's go; in my earliest recollection he was already almost fifty years old. Five-ten, 160 pounds, bald but for a few wisps of gray hair that I tried to smooth with spit-covered hands as I sat on his lap on the old Morrison recliner in the corner of the dining room. That is when I was able to beat the cat there; the moment Dad sat the family cat, whichever one it was, immediately jumped up on his lap. To my chagrin no matter what I did to get them to stay on my lap they instantly leapt to the floor.

When Daddy stood, a large bulge was clearly visible in his lower abdomen. It was an extremely advanced hernia that he refused to have repaired until it ruptured and nearly killed him. Daddy never took the time to take care of himself; he was too busy working. Sadly, no matter how much he tried he couldn't make an adequate living even for our minimal life style.

As bad as things were, he was quick with a joke for visitors as well as the family. When I complained that I wasn't physically developing as quickly as my friends and even some girls on the block who were younger, Dad quipped:

"Go over to the gas station; I saw a sign that said 'Flats fixed free' they'll take care of you"

He was, at the same time, exceedingly serious about world politics. I could always count on him to help me with compositions, especially dealing with current affairs. When I read his report verbatim in an economics class, Mrs. Lerner asked "who wrote that?" Caught off guard and red faced, I blurted: "My father." "Very good," she said, "but I would rather you write your own compositions in the future."

I tagged behind him like a puppy as he went around the house making necessary repairs, reinventing, designing and building devices or structures.

There was almost nothing he wouldn't undertake; his fixes weren't always cosmetically pleasing to the eye. He was a "form follows function" furniture repairer, inventor of an easy to push snow shovel that I couldn't budge and problem solver extraordinaire.

Major jobs beyond his scope of expertise, like painting the outside of the house, replacing or repairing shingles on the upper part of the house, reupholstering furniture, however, went undone. As a result, the outside of house, which had been painted every five or six years by the previous owners who first removed all the old paint, was allowed to deteriorate. Inside, plaster cracked, walls became dirty as did floor coverings that we couldn't afford to repair or replace.

Socially, Daddy was a gracious host. At any given time, three-to-four neighbors, acquaintances, Benny's, Shirley's or my friends were in or around the house and he welcomed them all. Even when he came home after a long day at work, sometimes having his dinner with someone looking down his throat, he maintained a pleasant patter.

He was an avid reader and had a controversial perspective on almost any subject. He read the New York Times every morning on his way to work. When Shirley started taking the train to work she made believe she didn't know him because he had his own inimitable way of reading the oversized paper. Rather than fold it in half so as not to bother the riders to his left and right, Dad spread it wide open. When he finished an article he folded it in half the long way and several times in the other direction. He then used it as an arm rest, propping it upright on his thigh, placing his folded elbow on top of it and resting his chin on his hand while he contemplated what he had just read.

I learned from Aunt Nettie that when he was young he loved to read poetry; this supported Mama's complaints when they were on the farm:

"Some farmer you are, when you are supposed to be milking the cows for the milk pick-up you are sitting under a tree reading poetry."

Whenever the story came up, which was quite often, he confirmed it:

"That's true," he would declare, "I could get lost in Walt Whitman's world and forget about the time."

He enjoyed exploring different places; and not only vicariously through his reading. According to Aunt Nettie, before he was married he frequently disappeared from the family home in Brooklyn for weeks at a time. His parents and sisters worried that some calamity surely must have befallen him. But on each such occasion, he would turn up just as suddenly as he had vanished. Nettie recounted one instance as follows:

"One morning after Harry was gone about a week I passed his room and a foul smell floated through the open door. I peered inside and saw a strange man with long unkempt hair, fully clothed in outdoor garb, lying atop the bedding.

'I screamed out and Harry woke with a start.'

'What is it? Why are you screaming?'

'Who is that man in your bed, I asked cowering.'

'Oh, him, I found him downstairs when I got home last night. It was very cold so I brought him up to thaw out. Harry replied."

This outcome may have had less to do with his nomadic nature than his anomalous attitude toward strangers of any ilk; from the hapless street person to the stranded motorist in the middle of the night on a rural road to the odd collection of drifters, many quite bizarre, who frequented our house.

Welcoming as he was, he had some quirky intolerances toward certain ordinary behaviors. When he came home from a hard day's work to find us gathered around the radio engrossed in a mystery or responding to the canned laughter of a situation comedy he would bark:

"Turn that foolishness off, put on the news."

If one of us ooh'd or ah'd in telling a story he would exclaim: "no exclamations please!"

Dad had a hot temper but it took a lot to set it off. Bullying one of his children was a sure trigger. When our curmudgeonly next door neighbor chased Benny from his yard and warned that he would strike him and have him arrested if he ever climbed over his fence again, Dad came out, got in his face and growled:

"Don't you ever threaten my son or any of my children again or you will be one sorry man." The neighbor mumbled something about his property but quickly backed away and retreated into his house. Dad almost never lost his temper with Benny or me. When he so much as raised his voice an octave or two my tear ducts went into overdrive while Mamma could scream at me endlessly without eliciting a response.

Shirley, however, had her ways of setting off ferocious furies. In one case she so enraged Dad that he went to punch her, but at the last second put his fist through the kitchen window behind her instead; as a result he was unable to completely extend his middle finger on his right hand for the rest of his life. In another instance, he forbade her from getting into a car with a couple of guys about whom he had bad vibes. He then parked himself on the stoop blocking her exit. Out of nowhere she struck him on the head from behind. Stunned, he got up, grabbed her by the hair and dragged her into the house. Mamma wasn't home to halt the carnage; I cried, pleaded for mercy for Shirley and tried to pull him away from her. After a few minutes he stopped as if in a stupor and stumbled away. Shirley got up off the floor unhurt, physically at least, and stormed out of the house.

It was hard to believe that this was the same man that we, Shirley more than anyone, called for when we were sick; the one who often came home from work to be with us. The Dad who comforted us while the doctor gave us antibiotic shots in our buttocks' while Mamma paced back and forth in the basement, too nervous to watch; the same Dad who took the train every Sunday for several months to a veteran's hospital in Pennsylvania to visit Benny.

Indeed, Dad mellowed. The older he became the longer hours he worked and the more Mama worried about him. By 10:00PM when we went to look for him we watched as he trudged up the hill from the station. We could always tell it was him by the slightly hunched back, weary gate and smoke rising from the wet Camel butt dangling from his mouth that no doubt had a long ash precariously dangling from its tip. Close-up his gentle powder blue eyes smiled when he saw us coming toward him, revealing a few remaining tobacco stained teeth.

He gently chastised us for worrying about him. At home, no matter how late it was, Mama had something ready for him to eat. Despite the hardships and quarrels, he was her partner and best friend until his death after thirty-six years of marriage.

To his children he was a caring, nurturing mentor when we let him be. To friends and visitors he was loyal and affable— always willing to lend a helping hand.

Regrettably the privation, struggles and friction caused by Dad's inability to provide the way he would have liked, something he lamented as he faced the end of his life, cast a shadow over the richness he brought to our lives.

Chapter 23
Mama

"Never judge a book by its cover" certainly applied to Mama. From as early as I can remember she looked some twenty years older than she was. By the time she reached her early forties her once strawberry blond hair turned salt and pepper, and became soft, silky snow-white in her fifties. She stood five feet tall and weighed 157 pounds for most of the time I remember.

A woman who, by all accounts, had cared very much about her person when she was young, Mama totally disregarded her personal needs; her hair and clothing were unkempt; her face deeply wrinkled, and her cheeks hollow from the loss of her teeth. She had lost her upper pearly whites in her early forties supposedly because I, who nursed until I was a year and a half old, sapped her of her calcium — talk about guilt. For several years she wore a natural looking upper plate. However, when she lost her bottom teeth a few years later and did not replace them, there was nothing to anchor her upper denture.

"What a cute granddaughter you have," passersby remarked gesturing to me.

"Is this your daughter?" they asked about Mrs. Eifler just ten years her junior.

Mama smiled but a small flicker in her eyes indicated that her feelings were hurt. She often pined for her early years in America when she was, as most young women, very conscientious about her appearance, buying trendy dresses, suits and hats. After the farm and living hand to mouth for years, she had given up. She wore old housedresses, worn shoes and no bra. Sometimes a smudge of soot or garden soil dotted her face or lodged under her fingernails.

Behind this exterior was a person vitally interested in family, friends and the world. Housework played second fiddle to reading and discussing current events. Mama applied the proverbial "nose to the grindstone" to her reading. She put her nose right up to the newspaper or magazine, closed one eye and perused article after article. We pleaded with her to get her eyes checked but she refused. In her later years when I took her to an ophthalmologist, at the direction of her doctor, he inquired:

"So, Mrs. Beck, did you ever wear eyeglasses?"

"No," she replied, "Thank God I never needed glasses, I always had good eyes."

He didn't quite agree and made her a pair of glasses.

When we finally got a TV, well after the rest of the world, she sat up real close and watched the news with passion, waving her fists at the political spin and its spinners. Today, I find myself similarly talking back to the boob tube.

Despite her broad interests Mama was naïve about some things. Soon after we moved to Daly Avenue and she befriended Mrs. Eifler, she unknowingly engaged in an illegal activity. Mrs. Eifler liked to play the numbers – she placed bets on numbers she dreamt – and Mama became a runner. She took the bets to Frank's barber shop in our old neighborhood.

"Do you know what you are doing? You could go to jail!" Dad yelled.

"Really? How can I say no? She's my best friend." Mama replied.

This would-be criminal, however, spent the greatest part of her time caring for us, shopping at the butcher, the grocer, the produce store around the corner. Food was a top priority; there was usually an abundance of fresh fruit, vegetables and dairy products in the ice box. I don't remember ever being hungry. Dinner at our house was rarely a family affair. Mama prepared personal favorites and served them at everyone's convenience.

"When I have a family I will not run a restaurant; everyone will eat whatever I cook and they will eat it at the same time," my sister declared time and again. As I recall she didn't follow through.

Mama never sat down at the table with us, opting instead for our leftovers after making sure everyone had enough to eat.

Looking after our welfare was a top priority, even when we rejected her efforts. Over my objections long after I was old enough to walk to school on my own she insisted on taking me to and fro. On one such occasion we saw Walter, a neighbor who is exactly one year older than I. We share a birthday and still exchange greetings to this day. On that day, a man was intimidating him. Mama immediately intervened, yelled at the perpetrator and chased him off.

"Leave him alone," she said to the man. "Walk away now! And never come back here."

"You, Walter, go to school. I'll watch you."

Walter remembers the incident fondly. It was not uncommon for Mama to intercede in altercations even among adults without regard to potential risk to herself.

Mama monitored our progress in school. Although she felt self-conscious about her lack of command of the English language she helped me with homework. She held up many a flash card to prepare me for spelling tests and helped me master the times tables by constant drilling. When it came to school, Shirley gave her a run for her money by getting her called to school for teacher conferences.

Mama was perhaps most anxious about Benny's schooling; the thinking was that as a male he would have to support a family someday. She also worried about the draft; aside from the angst commonly associated with war, her perception of troop treatment was colored by the way Jewish soldiers were abused in the Russian army. Moreover, she had an intuition that something bad would happen to him in a military environment.

That's why when Benny was about to graduate from high school and was interested in a career in animal husbandry, Mom was ecstatic. She went all out to make sure he went to an agricultural college so he would be exempt for the four years of his education and eligible for occupational exemption if he worked in farming, considered an essential field.

Despite her best intentions he ultimately was drafted into the Marines and soon after suffered a nervous breakdown, a devastating development for Mama.

When it came to her children, she was constantly nervous about one thing or another. She couldn't bear even the most common childhood diseases. She paced the basement when the doctor visited leaving Dad in charge. She literally ran several blocks to fetch the doctor at the first sign of illness. My chronic tonsillitis frequently accompanied by 105 degree temperatures kept both her and the doctor on the run. She arranged for and took me for tonsillectomies on several occasions only to return home, my tonsils in tact, unable to leave me overnight.

A chronic worrier, Mama always imagined the worst. She never went to sleep until everyone was home.

"How can you go to sleep when she's still not home; what if something happened to her, where can she be so late?, she chided Dad.

"Don't worry, she knows where she is; if anything happened you would hear, bad news travels fast." he would mutter half asleep.

She fretted about him too; when he was late coming home.

She was anxious when she didn't hear from Benny for long periods; she agonized over Shirley always, and later she lost sleep over what was happening with the grandchildren.

Hazy images appear almost daily. Mama laughing like a teenager, singing a Yiddish song or demonstrating Russian dances she did as a young girl. I find myself quoting her, reminiscing about the amusing things she said and her continuous counsel.

Just recently I spoke with Brenda, a childhood friend about Mama's concern that she, my younger playmate, always took the lead when we played house.

"Why is she always the mother, bossing you around?" Mama would ask angrily. She worried that I was too passive, and afraid my lack of aggressiveness would affect me negatively in the long run. She taught me manners and respect for others, but at the same time didn't want me to be a pushover. I often wonder how my life would be different if I weren't so accommodating and compromising, then and now.

Mama repeatedly told us things like:

"If someone holds out a hand, put some money in it. Many won't really need it, but since you can't know who truly does, it is better to make a mistake on the side of kindness. Never turn anyone away who needs a place to stay or food to eat."

Both Mom and Dad taught by example. Although we were poor, they were the first to help neighbors who had less, or fell on hard times.

They also had very similar feelings about religion. Disillusioned about it in their youth, persecuted simply because of it, they viewed religious doctrine as a divider of people. As such, they feared for their children, lest someday we too could suffer just because we were Jewish.

That's not to say that the traditions and beliefs associated with Judaism weren't discussed often in our home; Dad was well versed in the bible and attended synagogue on many high holy days when he had the price of a ticket. But they advocated assimilation in the hope that we would be spared the detrimental effects of discrimination and sincerely believed in equality.

Despite this, the message that came across loud and clear in our family was what I consider the very essence of religion: *Be good to your fellow man, help others whenever possible, and be honest and just in your dealings with others.*

My friends were often surprised when they met my parents. They were older than they expected. Mama, shoulders stooped by years of hardship, hollow cheeks and somewhat sad looking eyes, topped by wavy white hair looked much older than her years.

Yet, just a little time spent with her unmasked a woman who thought young and talked easily with them about any subject. Besides being a Bing (she called him Bill) Crosby fan, she liked Elvis while her peers were appalled at his "obscene" gyrations. She was a sucker for a good-looking actor like Robert Mitchum, Cary Grant and Paul Newman, and she laughed heartily at Bob Hope, George Burns and Milton Berle. Like a school girl when she started giggling she often couldn't stop.

Perhaps the most memorable aspect of Mama was her "funniness," especially the unintentional kind. Like most immigrants she used a lot of expressions from her native language. Yiddish is full of vivid idiomatic expressions — some wise, others downright nasty — most with a unique humorous quality that is not literally translatable.

I remember an incident when, at my urging, she walked, heel-to-toe, on the brick border of our small garden, quickly lost her balance, fell and sprained her ankle. When daddy returned home from work she was sitting on the back porch with her foot up on a chair. Her ankle was twice its normal size. Daddy was alarmed and asked her what had happened. She expressed her anger and frustration with me:

"The *roita choleryeh*" (red headed cholera or plague), one of her angry names for me, "made me walk on the bricks and I fell." Since I was only about seven at the time Dad wondered out loud:

"how could she *make* you to do such a silly thing, she's only seven." to which Mama had no response.

Wisdom, too, was often transmitted through the Yiddish vernacular. She counseled me not to speak too much because I would eventually say something stupid:

"*As me redt tsi feel, redtmen oise ah narishkeit.*" Consequently, to this day people can't figure out whether I am wise as in "still waters run deep," or too stupid to take part in a conversation.

As I get older I find myself saying things like *Az men lebt, derlebt men zich*, loosely translated to "if you live long enough you will experience everything – good and bad."

My friends are amused by these expressions that just pop out of my mouth at almost the right time. We are the last generation to laugh and learn from the humor and wisdom rooted in the Yiddish language; for some it immediately conjures images of their immigrant parents.

Mama was in many ways a typical "Jewish Mother," a term that has come to be associated with overbearing, overprotective, smothering mothers of all faiths. For example, although she never sat down to eat with us, she consistently urged us to eat: *"Ess, ess mon kind"* (pronounced as in *kick*), which means "eat, eat, my child."

So strong was her concern that I get enough nutrition, I still shudder at the flavor and stench of tonics and cod-liver oil she shoved down my throat to stimulate my appetite.

Mama's Jewish cooking wasn't exactly gourmet except for a few specialties like Kreplach (similar to ravioli and wontons), Gefilte fish, and the rock-hard sugar cookies.

I remember making fun of Mama every time I try to read something or thread a needle without my glasses.

I remember Mama for a lesson she taught me, an expression, an inspiration, a shared laugh or cry, something that irked me about her, or vice-versa. Her picturesque parlance punctuated by humor, insight, and sagacity got her messages across.

Even as she lay in a hospice bed, days before passing away, she made us laugh. As cancer consumed her liver allowing toxins to invade her brain she began to speak gibberish. Some of it was directed at the women of the Bible – Rebecca, Leah, and Ruth whom she had abandoned a long time before but recently rediscovered. This made Shirley and I wonder if her closeness to death opened a different communication channel. When a Priest tried to comfort her, Mama politely shooed him away.

"Thank you," she whispered, "but I don't have patience for this now."

Shirley and I speculated that she might prefer talking to a rabbi so we arranged a visit. The Rabbi came and no sooner did he begin to speak, did Mom, as diplomatically as she could, say:

"thank you for coming, but I don't have patience for this now."

From time to time, while I didn't do it often enough when I had the opportunity, I thank Mama for her exceptional devotion, wisdom, and patience with me.

Mama was a walking contradiction: at once brave yet fearful; affable but aggressive when necessary and sensible despite losing her cool and pacing in the basement when she was particularly nervous.

Days before the end of her life she was remorseful about her fears. She expressed sorrow for failures she attributed to them, for disappointment and opportunities lost because of them and she implored us not to let fear and insecurity diminish the quality of our lives.

Chapter 24
Big Brother

"Why did he get those beautiful eyelashes; it's not fair; I'm the girl" Shirley whined incessantly. Mother-nature had endowed Benny with long curly eyelashes that were the envy of all of her girlfriends.

Most of them had crushes on the almost six feet tall, trim 165 pound teenager. Those long lashes were capped off by nicely arched thick brows that almost touched in the middle and a mane of wavy dark brown hair. It wasn't unusual for him to rewet his hair three or four times before he sculpted a perfect groove in a flawless pompadour. Twinkling chocolate eyes and a quick shy smile endeared him to people of all ages and genders. He had a big group of friends, some almost as good looking as he.

Two years his junior Shirley's friends hung around our house whenever possible to get a glimpse of Benny and perhaps catch his eye. They blushed and giggled when he walked in. He grinned timidly and quickly grabbed a Spaldeen, football or basketball and rushed out for a game of stickball, touch football, or to throw hoops at the schoolyard.

If they were just hanging out on the block sometimes they let me join them.

"Show the guys how you whistle," he would coax me.

I would purse my lips and blow, and blow without making a sound.

"Wow," they would laugh; "you taught her good."

He also taught me how to make a peach-pit ring by rubbing the pit on any and all cement surfaces until it was smooth all over and the seed was visible. Then remove the soft seed, and shape the top of the pit into a square flat surface and carve your initials.

He and his friends liked to play "monkey in the middle." Two of them stood about twenty feet apart and threw a ball to each other, well over my head (I was always the monkey) as I jumped up and tried unsuccessfully to catch it.

They couldn't get rid of me that easily. I enjoyed whatever they did as long as they paid attention to me. Benny was a very attentive big brother. He played with me whenever he was home. He shadow boxed with me. He demonstrated how to block punches by putting his arms in front of his face. Then have me set myself up. Next he'd throw a punch and stop just short of touching me. Then we switched and I tried to strike back. He found it particularly amusing to simply hold the top of my head with one hand as I flailed recklessly at the air.

He also taught me how to tell time on the clock he made expressly for that purpose.

To get Mama into the act, he lifted me onto his shoulders and ducked under doorways. "Stop!" she screamed, "you'll hurt her."

We laughed as Mama flinched each time he bent down just in time to spare my head.

He patiently played checkers, monopoly and casino with me and showed me the finer points of gin rummy.

He continued to miss the farm so much that when it was time to go to high school he found the only one in New York City that offered an "Agricultural" program. Newtown High School in Elmhurst, Queens had a small farm and a few animals. At the age of thirteen, he travelled approximately two hours by a series of trains and a half-mile walk each way to and from school Monday through Friday. He was up at 6:00AM and didn't arrive home until 5:00PM. Come summer the school arranged for students in the agricultural program to work on a farm usually in upstate New York. He was finally back in his element.

In 1950, however, one year before graduation, the Korean War threatened to disrupt his young life. For the first time since World War II, the "draft" was reinstated.

This scared the hell out of Mama; Benny would surely be drafted. She was happy when he applied to several agricultural colleges where he could pursue his interest in animal husbandry. He was accepted at National Agricultural College in Doylestown, Pa.

One morning, a month before he was scheduled to leave, I woke up with a swollen face. I remembered that the day before I was hit in the face by a wayward ball in front of our house during a stickball game. Mama applied ice but it was too late for that. Aspirin would surely take down the swelling. The problem was that I could not swallow pills. So once again, big brother came to the rescue.

"Just put the aspirin on the back of your tongue like this," he demonstrated. " Then take a sip of water and swallow."

I placed the aspirin as indicated, swallowed the water and voila the aspirin was still there. He tried again and again, swallowing aspirins every time. He consumed at least a dozen. Each time I tried, my aspirin stayed on my tongue and my face remained swollen.

After several days, Mama took me to the doctor who quickly diagnosed "Mumps."

Unfortunately Benny soon had it too. It was a perfect example of the adage: "No good deed goes unpunished." Seventeen is the worst possible time for a young man to contract this virus. In men and teenage boys it often results in an inflammatory condition that can cause swelling in one or both testicles and more important, it can cause sterility. Unfortunately for Benny, the former happened and it was very painful for some time. Thankfully, he was cured in time to start school in September, as planned. And, as for Mumps possibly causing sterility, I breathed a sigh of relief at the birth of each of his four children.

Once he left home at seventeen, except for short visits, we hardly saw him. He received his Bachelor's Degree in Animal Husbandry, worked in the field for some time, served a short tour in the Marines, married and raised a family all in Pa.

Although contact was far too limited, there was something about Benny that made you feel that you just saw him yesterday. The whole family would just melt as soon as we laid eyes on his warm twinkling eyes and fluttering eye lashes.

Chapter 25
Big Sister

At 5'2" and 125 pounds for most of her life, Shirley was anything but average. She was precocious, bright, and talented. In addition to being a guy magnet, her big expressive brown eyes concealed a mysterious personality – kind yet sometimes callous and exceptionally creative nonetheless somewhat damaging to those close to her and, most important, to herself.

In many ways she was my role model. I envied her many talents and looked up to her. Sister relationships, however, are often complex. Ours could be turbulent and harmonious, loving and loathsome, symbiotic and adversarial – all at the same time. Shirley had the unique ability to go from affectionate playful big sister, tickling me until I almost convulsed with laughter to abruptly reducing me to tears.

She never got over my crashing into her world and making her the *middle* child. Her disappointment endured; ten years after my birth she continued to rebel. When I cried in my carriage while she jumped rope, she turned the carriage so my eyes faced directly into the sun to shut me up.

"Pretty soon you closed your eyes and dozed off," she recalled with a smile.

She helped me with school projects, from flour and water three-dimensional landscapes and masks, to an elaborate family tree using India ink on oak tag to trace my red hair, not to mention my eighth-grade graduation dress – without her help I might still be there.

Shortly after we moved into the house, I tumbled down a full flight of stairs and two giant bumps formed on my forehead; word was that I didn't just fall. Although she vehemently denied it, everyone believed she pushed me. I don't remember the incident, but unfortunately for her, and me, the physical evidence remained until I was twelve when my bulging brow finally receded.

I doubt that she deliberately pushed me down those steps but there was evidence that she derived a devious delight from my physical or emotional pain.

"We found you in a garbage can," she often chided. "Didn't you ever wonder why you are the only one in the family with red hair?"

She was referring to my thick, curly, red mop which became a torture chamber in her hands.

"Does that really hurt," she cynically reacted to my "ouches," moans and tears as she tugged the comb through countless knots.

Yet, she also showed love and affection. When I was sick, which was often with chronic tonsillitis, I'd hear her come home from work and anxiously inquire:

"How's the baby?"

She brought me candy, comics and cut-outs to help me pass the time.

She bought me things for my birthday, holidays and often just because she thought about me. But when she got upset with me about something she demanded the immediate return of something she had given me:

"Give me back my watch," she would demand; it could have been "my dress" or "my ring" or anything to make me feel indebted to her.

For my graduation from eighth-grade she took the day off from work, bought me a wrist corsage made up of a single orchid with a big bow and cheered me on. More important if it wasn't for her help and know-how I would not have been able to finish my dress. We had to make our own and I was all thumbs when it came to sewing. She took lots of pictures to mark the event, most celebratory; one, however, shows me sitting on the back porch in my white dress sobbing; it was as if she had to dampen her kindness. Although I have no recollection of what precipitated my unhappiness, clearly she took some pleasure in preserving it.

As a student herself, with a 128 IQ (Intelligence Quotient) much higher than mine, just two points below the top range, her grades were generally close to the bottom of the norm. IQ scores were very significant in determining courses of study, class placement and, by their nature, expectations. As was true in most cases, Shirley turned the latter upside down.

She showed no interest in school, allied herself with friends who shared her standards and seemed to have serous self-esteem issues. Her underperformance was the subject of frequent calls for Mama to go to school to speak to teachers and administrators.

One French teacher complained:

"Forget college, if she got a job in sanitation she would sweep the debris from the streets back onto the sidewalks. It's a shame that with her IQ she may not graduate from high school. You and your husband have to do something to make her understand the importance of a high school diploma."

That statement turned out to be prophetic. She completed four years of high school short one credit to earn her diploma. Mama and Daddy were devastated; if Shirley was, she didn't show it. "I'll get a job as a hairdresser," she declared.

"With your brains that's what you want to do? You want to listen to the "yentas" (Yiddish for gossiping women) all day? You can do better than that. Maybe you should go to secretarial school."

Shirley was livid; she thought Mama was ruining her life, a belief that stayed with her from then on.

She managed to find work as a file clerk in a small manufacturing company. Applications to major insurance companies, AT&T and Con Edison met with religious discrimination. In 1949 Jews still faced overt prejudice in large companies, sports clubs and other organizations. Nevertheless, she worked and contributed to the household.

Soon after she started she installed our first phone – one of the last homes to do so. Later she bought our first refrigerator for the upstairs kitchen to replace one of the last iceboxes still in use. She added a small gas range and thanks to her Mama no longer had to cook in the basement; she prepared meals in the kitchen and we ate in the dining room.

Shirley's hands could fabricate anything her eyes saw. She made a lot of clothing for herself, me and others. If she saw a dress she liked, she created her own patterns by simply looking at it; she'd cut and sew an exact replica. She was meticulous about herself and her clothing, washing and ironing every Sunday in preparation for the following week.

Around the house she painted, decorated and bought little knick knacks. She patiently cut perfect petals from colored crepe paper, wrapped wire with green paper and glued the petals one-by-one to form bouquets of tulips.

In my teens it was Shirley, not Mama who I turned to with questions about physical changes, sex, relationships and she was always ready with answers.

When she was in a giddy mood we'd have "gibberish" conversations in which we said absolutely nothing in a wide variety of accents. It drove Mama mad – but we, especially I, laughed hysterically – until suddenly she would snap:

"OK that's it. That's enough." and the game was over.

There was nothing she could do or say to stop me from wanting to be with her. If she put up a fuss about taking me along with her and her friends to the park, the movie or the ice cream parlor, Mama appealed to her:

"Why don't you let her come; she just wants to be with you."

"Why do I always have to take her? I just want to be with my friends"

"Don't you see? She loves you, she looks up to you?"

Most of the time she acquiesced, which wasn't always good for her; sometimes from the corner of my eye, I'd catch her and a date steal a kiss in the movie and couldn't wait to get home and tattle.

When she was eighteen she met, fell in love and married Billy. He was quite handsome in his tight dungarees and black leather motorcycle jacket on a 6'2" tall thin frame. With piercing blue eyes and dark brown wavy hair, he looked like a young Clint Eastwood and James Dean wrapped into one.

Their courtship and eight-month marriage that ended in an annulment was a nightmare for her and the entire family. Once it was over all the problems and the entire situation was forgotten and rarely if ever discussed.

She ultimately returned home and went on to have several relationships. One long-term one with a neighbor across the street went on for years before she had her heart broken when Walter was drafted, stationed in Germany and married a woman he met there. She continued to live at home and contribute to the household needs and improvements until she met and married Gerry in 1956.

When she was happy she was the most fun person to be with but when she was angry she was callously insensitive. When she wanted to, she could sweet talk the devil, but when she felt wronged she would call down evil upon her perceived wrongdoer, bellowing expletives, profanity and condemnations.

Our relationship went through lots of changes over time. Her dominance diminished as our chronological age difference became less significant. As adults we shared confidences, reminiscences and day-to-day chats. We disagreed often, mostly about how she dealt with her children.

She had a standard response to any comment I might make about her parenting. Whether I criticized a light smack or moving them out of state disrupting the kids' school, she sarcastically replied:

"Sure," she would say, "you know exactly how to raise kids! You did a great job," a charge I could not argue having not raised any biological children of my own. Nevertheless it hurt because I intuitively knew that her action would be detrimental and I sincerely cared.

After the family settled in Tennessee where Gerry took a job with TVA in the early seventies, we talked almost daily; argued, laughed and cried. Too often one wrong word, in what started out as a heart-to-heart, led to a short period of not talking. Within a week, one of us always broke down and called as if nothing happened and routine calls resumed.

From my birth until her death in December 1999, at the age of 68, our relationship remained a combination of contention and acquiescence, laughter and tears, fallings-out and mutual love and caring. Sadly, I don't think she ever understood how much she meant to me.

Chapter 26
Baby Sister

An overriding sense that I had while growing up was that I was small and irrelevant. No doubt, at the same time my family position as the baby had its benefits. The big age differences between my siblings and me probably gave me the edge on learning things like how to tell time, play cards, board games as well as some less desirable stuff earlier than my peers. Still I couldn't wait to be grown up like everyone else in the family and in some ways I was.

Long before I should have been, I was aware and worried about grown up problems along with the everyday difficulties of childhood. While most children are concerned about something happening to a parent; I was obsessed. Beside their advanced age, Mama and Daddy argued all the time – sometimes it looked like they might hurt or kill each other if I didn't stand between them, a hand on both their chests. I worried that they might divorce in which case I would lose at least one of them. The worst part was that I felt powerless to change anything.

I couldn't move the clock forward to alter the dates of my parents' births so I wouldn't be embarrassed when they were mistaken for my grandparents. Nor could I stop the humiliation of loud quarrels the neighbors heard between them and Shirley when she became difficult for them to control. I wasn't able to buy myself nice clothing and wash and iron it so I wouldn't feel so self-conscious, ashamed and different. I certainly could not pay back taxes or mortgage interest to avoid losing the house and becoming homeless.

I often wonder if it is true that we are born with our basic personality traits: happy or sad, introvert or extrovert, anxious or carefree. If I had been shielded from some of the difficulties, would I have been a worrier anyway? In the few early family photos that have survived it seems like I was born to worry. In one of me in a carriage I look like the weight of the world was on my shoulders – it depicts a sad squinty eyed chubby baby looking warily at the camera; another shows a grim-faced four-year-old with long curls seemingly trying to recede into the brick wall behind her.

Mom had spent hours on those ringlets that were carrot-colored, matched by a face full of freckles that also populated the skin on my arms and legs. Dull hazel, sometimes green, eyes and a small gap between slightly bucked front teeth completed the picture. No wonder I looked so unhappy.

Some three years after the latter photo was taken, at about seven or eight, I started to take steps to accelerate the aging process to facilitate catching up with the rest of the family. When we had breakfast together on weekends, I demanded,

"I want coffee too,"

No problem, Daddy put a drop of the tantalizing brew in my milk from then on. About the same time I began to beat everyone to the basement kitchen on Saturday and Sunday morning to put the coffee up. While it percolated, I lit up one of Daddy's cigarettes, stood at the back door and puffed away. Like Daddy (and Bill Clinton), I did not inhale — yet.

At every opportunity I tried to wear Shirley's grown up clothes even if it was way to big on me. On more than one such occasion she attempted to strangle me with a neckerchief or blouse that she had carefully washed and ironed.

When I was a teenager, not at all popular with the boys, I asked Shirley:

"How come so many boys like you?"

"You have to flirt with them," she replied. "First look at them," she demonstrated staring into my eyes. "Then smile like you like what you see."

We laughed when I lamely tried to mimic her sexy come hither look only to resemble Daffy Duck.

I had a few boyfriends in the neighborhood; Dickie McGee was the first to attempt a kiss and we were both surprised at my response. Al Glass — AKA "Tiny" at 6'2" and 250 pounds when he was thirteen, started hanging around when he returned from Florida where he was sent to recover from Scarlet fever — and we became an item for some time.

Arnie moved across the street when I was thirteen. I admired him from afar. When we were about seventeen we became quite close for a time.

Through the years I had blind dates for which I'd often wished I was indeed blind. Like single young women of the time I also went to dances and singles bars — both of which brought out the worst in people most of whom were usually on the defensive.

It wasn't until I graduated from high school and entered the workforce that I started to become the real me. I began to feel a sense of self. I was reinforced by doing well at my job. Through my contribution to household expenses, conflicts subsided. In addition, conditions improved more with the conversion to gas heat and hot water – no more coal and wood boxes. Soon we made necessary repairs, painted the house inside and out.

I enjoyed some of the perks of life in New York City; saw the best of Broadway, dined in excellent restaurants and took fun trips with friends. Except for still not finding a life partner, life was good. I also began to take business classes at night at City College of New York to advance at my job. Things were looking up.

Before long, what promised to be a nice life, was marred by Dad's illness, first with prostate and hernia surgeries and then with his death when I was twenty-five. Mom and I continued to live in the house. Soon the neighborhood began to decay. Four years later Mom too became ill and had surgery which appeared at the time to have been successful.

I continued to work and go to school at night, going out with friends and vacationing here and there. Eventually, based on a wise suggestion from a good friend, I put my education in full gear, finally getting a Bachelor's degree in Business Administration in January, 1969 at the ripe old age of thirty. The hard work was worth it. It enhanced a career I enjoyed for almost thirty years, helped us jump to a middle-class lifestyle and gave me a feeling of accomplishment.

I often think about my resolve, self assurance and doggedness all things considered.

Shirley sometimes exhibited resentment toward me, seemingly for trying to make life better.

"Sure you have a college degree – you know everything," she would announce misperceiving a look or simple statement as negative.

There was no way I could dissuade her from thinking I looked down on her. This could not have been further from the truth. For most of my life I had looked up to her. If she sensed anything from a look or a word it may have been that I felt a bit let down that life had not treated her and the whole family better.

Chapter 27
Pets are Players Too

Animals were always a major part of our lives. We always had a cat whose job it was to keep the house free of mice. Truth be told I think they brought more home than they dissuaded from coming in or executed. Not to mention other critters like the birds, rat and squirrel carcasses they dragged in.

Tiger was in fact most responsible for the purchase of the house and he deservedly benefited from the move. For him it was a "win-win." He had full run of the house and direct access to the outside. He quickly learned to stand by the door and rub against it. If no one was near, he signaled us with his –

"I want out' meow." As a last resort he scratched the door feverishly.

To reenter he jumped on an outside windowsill and waited patiently until we got the message and let him in. Several times a day Mama called him home. No matter where he was, he came running the minute he heard her refrain:

"Here kitty, kitty, kitty."

The only sound he answered more quickly was the call of the wild. Neutering and spaying were rare back then; we couldn't afford veterinarian care for our sick animals, let alone contraception. During mating season our feline Romeo became restless; he lurked near the door, rubbed against our legs, looked up at us and vehemently vocalized: "let me out, let me out, please." Outside, his gray and black marbled muscular body, John Wayne swagger and big jowls were ready to bite into the neck of a female in heat or fight off any and all competitors. The neighborhood was full of both. Daddy used to imitate the mating calls.

"Listen" he whispered his forefinger across his lips. "She moans 'Johhhhn' and he responds: 'Maaaaary"

Our "John" clearly enjoyed his share of love making. We never saw the other guy, but many nights Tiger dragged himself home, beat up, bedraggled, and bushed. He not only had to battle other Toms, but the females often swatted and scratched their significant others out of pain or perhaps pleasure. Either way, he licked his wounds, got some rest and before long he was back at it, using up what seemed to be more than his allotted nine lives in this manner.

When he was not on the prowl, Tiger adeptly climbed trees, chased squirrels and other unsuspecting critters and tormented mice.

Daddy thought Tiger was the smartest cat around; he attributed much of his intellect and agility to the six toes on his front paws. Many believe that polydactyl cats, as they are called, are able to perform feats of manual dexterity because they have two opposing digits on each paw comparable to human thumbs.

Besides being an excellent climber, creature chaser and mouser, Tiger was a fair pianist. During the night he serenaded us by walking back and forth on the keyboard. Daddy wasn't the only person enamored by a polydactyl cat. Ernest Hemingway surrounded himself with them while writing in his Key West, Florida home. As a result cats with this genetic anomaly are also called "Hemingway cats." Generations of Hemingway's menagerie still wander the grounds of his home which is now a tourist attraction. I met a number of them when I visited a few years ago. They continue to be pampered and multiply.

Ironically, Tiger's procreation days were cut short by his carousing. He limped home after a night out on the town, his tail ripped open, body scratched and right eye turned inside out. A few days later I came home from school and Tiger was gone; Daddy had taken him to the ASPCA to put him out of his misery.

Some months before Tiger's demise he almost had a playmate. Daddy was tinkering around in front of the house when he noticed a man and his dog walking back and forth across the street looking at him each time he passed. He was a small man, about 5'2" tall, a bit stooped from age or depression, or both. Heeling obediently beside him, the dog, who looked like a Doberman mix, tan and black, ears pointing up, came up to the man's hip. Finally they crossed the street and approached Daddy:

"You just moved in right?"

"Yes, several months ago."

"You have a family, yes?

"A wife, three kids and a cat."

"I wish I had a family. This is my dog Sport, he's my only family. The problem is I'm getting too old to care for him. We live in a small apartment around the corner and he's a big dog; he needs exercise. He's wonderful with children. He doesn't cost much to keep, eats scraps of whatever I eat. And, he is a good watch dog. Maybe you would like to take him."

"I don't think so" Daddy respectfully declined. "This is a pretty small house. The cat may not be happy with a dog coming into his territory. Besides, you look like you are very fond of your dog."

"I am. I just can't take care of him anymore. You would do me a big favor if you took him."

Dad reluctantly agreed and coaxed Sport into the yard. His master walked toward home, head hung low, the dog's eyes following him. Daddy tried to make friends with the dog. He brought some water out in a bowl. Sport tried to take a few sips but he was distracted. He kept looking in the direction the old man had gone. This went on for about an hour. Then the dog became restless, walking back and forth. Daddy saw the man walk slowly up the block. As he approached Sport jumped up, put his paws on his master's shoulders nearly knocking him over.

"How is he doing?" the man asked petting him as the dog's tongue lapped his face all over.

"He's very upset, keeps looking for you," Daddy responded.

"I'm concerned too; I thought I better tell you a little more about him. I do actually feed him a few specialties. Every morning for breakfast I make him two scrambled eggs. For dinner he likes a steak. I walk him three times a day, sometimes four — he needs lots of exercise."

"Oh! We can't afford to feed a dog like that; I have five mouths to feed. Besides, I'm not home to walk him so often and my wife is busy with the house. Maybe you should take him back. I can see you two love each other very much and we are not really in a position to keep him."

"OK, thank you for your trouble," the man replied without missing a beat. He and his dog, both looking just a little bit taller, set out for home. Dad beamed as he watched them walk away.

Bitten (no pun intended) by the bug, a short time later Daddy presented me with a little white ball of fur on the morning of my sixth birthday. We named the puppy Tiny. Like babies of all species, Tiny was adorable, running around, playing and kissing everyone. Daddy started house-breaking him right away. Every two hours or so, he and I walked up and down the street with Tiny. He was such a nice addition to the household; even Mama warmed up to him despite the fact that she did not want another pet. All was well for about two weeks when Tiny became lethargic; his stomach was upset and he began to whimper. We put him in a box, and took him to the doctor. The doctor quickly diagnosed Distemper and advised Daddy to put the dog to sleep; the mortality rate for puppies was very high. Dad agreed. We brought Tiny's remains home, dug a grave in a corner of the backyard and conducted a small service.

A series of cats followed; none as extraordinary as Tiger. Although we were careful about gender, preferring males, somehow a few females snuck through; the only thing worse than an unaltered male is a female that has not been spayed. When they are in heat, they are single-minded about finding to mate to fertilize their eggs. They howled, yowled and squealed to get out. No sooner did we let them out, the Casanovas gathered round them and fought each other for the right to impregnate their prey. It was akin to a gang-bang. There was no keeping them in, but once they were out I cringed at the instant ruckus I heard. I could only imagine what they were doing to them. Our females also came home beaten and bruised. The end result, however, was priceless; I watched as one of our females delivered 6 little sacks, lick each kitten clean and hide them all in the closet for safe keeping.

When any of the large numbers of feral felines that stalked the streets and yards had litters they watched over them very carefully. If they saw us near them they picked them up in their teeth, one-by-one, and quickly moved to a different location One day my friends and I found a maturing litter in Lenny's yard. I picked one up and brought it up toward my face; it clawed the inside of my lip. Of course, Mama got all upset when she saw it. I was scheduled to go on a school trip the next morning. Instead I went to the doctor for a tetanus shot.

Then there was Blackie, a high strung black Spitz mix. His family moved away and left him homeless. Of course we took him in. Mistake. Blackie was about eighteen inches tall and some two feet long from his nose to a tail that curled up, with a fox-like head and shiny coat. He was full-grown which meant we couldn't train him – what you saw was what you got. He was very protective in a strange kind of way. When Mama's friends stopped by after shopping the dog welcomed them, bags and all. However, the instant they tried to leave with their bundles he barked and bore his teeth at them; if they chose to leave their packages they were free to go. He also protected Shirley in the morning when Mama tried to wake her in the little room on her wall-to-wall bed. Blackie lodged under the bed in the attack position and barked, growled and snarled with the ferocity of a wild wolf keeping Mama at bay. And when anyone fought in the house, he added to the shouting by jumping in between the parties and roaring like an angry lion.

Blackie's *bite* was worse than his *bark*. As time went by he nipped every member of the family. He never caused a lot of damage and this bad behavior was tolerated for months until he made the grave mistake of biting "the baby" – me. Poor Dad made another trip to the ASPCA. I don't know if Blackie was put up for adoption or euthanized but he no longer resided with us. It was back to felines for us.

Kemo was our last cat on Daly Avenue. He got his name from the oft repeated phrase Kemo Sabe, or "faithful friend." It was the phrase Tonto, a Native American scout always used to address the Lone Ranger who always wore a black mask over his eyes. Both were fictional characters in a popular TV show of the same name in the 50's. You guessed it – our Kemo was primarily white with a black saddle and black around his eyes. The most domesticated cat we ever had, he lived up to his name as a faithful friend to Mom and me.

When I was growing up, the minute Daddy sat on the recliner the cat, whichever one we had at the time, curled up on his lap. They all looked so serene there I only wanted them on my lap; the more I tried to force them the more they spurned me. Although the main reason we had them was to keep the mice away, some of their antics were quite entertaining. They involved toying with frightened mice that scurried around the house and drove Mama and Shirley out or on top of the round table screaming for help. In my tomboy days I came to their rescue. Later, I joined them.

More often than not our pets helped take the focus away from our problems. And, like the vast majority of pet owners, we considered them family.

Part IV
Family Matters—Circa 1940s and 1950s

Chapter 28
Tales of the Round Oak Table

Not a scratch could be found on the pristine oak table when we were first introduced to it. It didn't take long, however, before our captivating cast of characters sketched our indelible selves on its surface.

By the time we became the rightful owners of the furniture that belonged to the previous owners, we estimated that it was about sixteen years old. The dating process we employed was far from scientific, based solely on yellowed newspapers that lined the old linoleum floor coverings dated in 1928.

The forty-four inch circular table stood like a lioness in the center of the dining room. A turned pedestal, her four sturdy curved legs with precisely carved claw feet complete with their natural looking nails, supported the top surface. It was made up of two semi circles, their mirror-matched oak grain meeting perfectly in the middle; an extra leaf rested in a slot below. No doubt it was pampered by the three senior siblings who lived in the meticulously maintained house.

Enter our family of five – three children, ages five-to-fifteen, who had been crowded into a third-floor, two bedroom, walk-up apartment for four years – and the once coddled dining table instantly became a desk, game table, conference table, and an all around hangout for a wide variety of characters of all ages.

All three of us did our homework and school projects on it. It looked on as I drew a family tree with India ink on white oak tag that traced my red hair to Daddy and his family; it observed Mama helping me with arithmetic and spelling. It supported my composition book, as Dad sat in the Morrison recliner and dictated reports to me.

The table tolerated cigarette burns, spills as well as cuts and pricks when clothing patterns were pinned and cut on it. It served as a work bench when Daddy brought work home from the shop and we sat around it filling and closing pompoms.

Family and friends played monopoly, scrabble, checkers, casino, and rummy on it to pass the time. It patiently listened day in and day out while people gathered around it to talk, commiserate, and exchange experiences into the wee hours of the morning; it couldn't help but eavesdrop on religious discussions, many quite heated, as well as lots of idle gossip that perked the ears of a little girl who should not have poked her nose into grown-up conversations.

Twenty years later on Halloween morning in 1964 that child, now a grown woman of twenty-four, heard a spine-chilling scream from the dining room. I came down to see Mama looking on in terror as Dad, who had been suffering with a coronary condition for months, succumbed to a fatal heart attack while reading the Times at the table.

Yes, the round table became a cache of myriad moments – happy and sad, good and bad, devotion and dissention, new life and life lost.

After our once bustling household was reduced to just two of us, Mama spent months stripping and refinishing the once unsoiled preserver of the past. She removed years of food residue, ink marks, paint drops, gashes, burns, and scratches – even carved initials that left seemingly irreparable scars.

Using a variety of paint thinners, steel wool, and sandpaper Mama attacked the old finish. Coarse sandpaper helped smooth stubborn blemishes followed by fine sanding, several coats of Golden Oak stain and polish turned the clock back to the spring of 1944.

Today, the old oak table, a part of my life for more than six decades, stands in my kitchen. It is more than a little warped, the top halves don't quite meet anymore, and the thin veneer is coming away in a few places.

Now somewhat of a conversation piece, it is still at the center of activity, dishing up warmhearted meals and memories every day.

Chapter 29
Kindergarten Dropout

In September 1945 I finally made it. My fantasy of going to school like Benny and Shirley came true. I looked forward with great anticipation to kindergarten. Mama registered me in P. S. 6, the elementary school most of the kids on our block attended. Shirley had graduated from there many years before.

I was so happy. I chatted excitedly with neighborhood friends. Before I knew what was happening I realized that the teacher was angrily addressing me; she held up a key and barked:

"If you don't stop talking right now I will take this key and lock you in that closet," she gestured toward a door in the corner of the room.

Without uttering another word, I looked down and tried my hardest not to cry. When I heard the lunch bell, I jumped out of my seat and ran for the door.

I saw Mama at the base of the steps with a big smile on her face. No doubt she anticipated that I would report how much fun I had. One look at me and her radiant grin instantly turned to a fretful frown. Tears cascaded from my troubled eyes. She tried to console me.

"What happened?" She asked over and over.

"She was going to lock me in a closet," I sobbed.

"Why did she want to lock you up, what were you doing?"

"I was talking," I responded. "I'm never going back there."

"We'll talk about it. Please stop crying," she pleaded.

Somehow we made it through the night. The next morning Mama dragged me back to school. I cowered behind her as she confronted the teacher:

"Is it true you told Susie you would lock her in a closet with a key?" Mama asked incredulously.

"Yes, I told her several times to be quiet and she kept talking; I cannot conduct a class if children don't listen to me."

"But this was her first day. She didn't know she wasn't allowed to talk. Don't you think you were too hard on her?" Mama asked.

"No," she replied. "I did what I had to do!"

"Well, I'll have to see what I have to do," Mama said.

She took me by the hand and ushered me out of the building.

"I'm never going back there," I continued to whimper.

"We'll see," she quieted me.

That evening, she and Daddy talked it over. Given my distress and Mama's concerns about the teacher's attitude, as well as the fact that kindergarten was not compulsory, they agreed to let me sit it out.

I got to play a lot of "house" with Brenda, my first girlfriend in the neighborhood who was a year behind me in school, and a few others still at home.

When September rolled around again, however, I had to go to first grade. It was mandatory. Mama registered in P.S. 67 a few blocks in the other direction. On the first day she curled my hair, dressed me in a new dress and shoes and prayed that I would not greet her with tears at the end of the day.

Ms. Conklin seemed nice. I was too frightened to open my mouth, which pleased her; she mistook my silence for being "a good girl," as opposed to the few students who were "bad" because they talked when they weren't supposed to.

To make matters worse, she used corporal punishment to modify bad behavior. She washed the tongue of any child who said a "bad" word; thought nothing of using her 18-inch wooden ruler to whack the knuckles of unruly students who talked out of turn or to each other which brought back my kindergarten experience and played havoc with my nervous system.

Each morning I woke up with a belly ache that kept me home a few days of most weeks. On days that I did attend, Mama was almost always forewarned of my upset stomach by classmates who preceded me to the exit with the announcement: "Susie threw up today!"

I was promoted to second grade, which for some administrative reason, was combined with third grade that year. The teacher, Ms. Brennan, was very kind. She did not resort to physical discipline to control her seven year-old charges. I was still frightened, uncomfortable and silent. Eventually, however, the regurgitation routine slowed considerably and before long it stopped. My absences were still frequent, many as a result of chronic tonsillitis.

My silence and absences were too much for my fourth grade teacher, Miss. Flax. On open school day she told Mama:

"She's absent every Monday and Thursday and she never talks except to answer questions. I don't like children who talk too much, but Susan is too quiet.. There must be something wrong with her."

Mama, fighting her own fears and frustrations about this situation became defensive:

"Next time I'll make one to order for you." she snapped back.

This interchange saved my life. Miss. Flax saw no alternative but to put me in a special "opportunity class," established for the first time for kids with a variety of social problems.

It was there that I met Mrs. Timpson, a unique teacher who turned out to be just the angel that I and twenty plus other special needs students with a variety of problems needed. She was an affectionate, caring and creative confidence builder.

The standard curriculum took a back seat to building our self esteem. We delivered milk and cookies, prepared and distributed attendance sheets to the teachers, ran errands for Mrs. T. Those who had skills in math or grammar tutored others who needed help. We performed in class plays, made frequent tea parties for our parents, and just about everyone got a chance to be class president.

Before long, stutterers stopped stammering; kids who would undoubtedly be on Ritalin today (for ADHD) settled down, and I started to talk and take part in activities. Mrs. Timpson's success was nothing short of miraculous.

When Mama attended open school day, Mrs. Timpson suggested that I didn't belong in the opportunity class.

"She's fine," she said. "I'm going to put her in a mainstream sixth grade class,"

"Please, I would appreciate it if you could keep her." This is the first time she is enjoying school — she is anxious to go even when she doesn't feel well," Mama pleaded on my behalf. Mrs. Timpson complied.

At my sixth grade Graduation I stood tall, at least as tall as possible, given that I led the girls, size-order procession. During the proceedings I walked proudly to the podium when my name was called to accept a surprise "citizenship" award. It was a pendant about the size of a half-dollar with the statue of "Justice" embossed on one side and my name along with the date inscribed on the other.

It was a day I would always remember as a defining moment in my life. It marked the end of seven traumatic years for this kindergarten dropout, now ready for a new start.

Chapter 30
Room to Let

Mama prominently displayed the sign in the living room window: "Room to Let-Inquire within"

As if the variety of characters that found their way to our house wasn't enough, we also invited a series of other sojourners to live with us for a fee.

Despite already tight living quarters, in 1946 when Benny went off to college, renting his room was part of the plan to help pay his tuition. Our first roomers were the Nicklesbergs.

Nick, one of thousands of returning veterans and his attractive bride, Lee needed a place to stay until they could find more adequate housing. He was the kind of guy who instantly made you feel like you knew him all of your life. They quickly made themselves at home.

The rental did not include meals or kitchen privileges. That didn't stop Nick. The first thing he did was check out the icebox, make a pot of coffee, and enjoy a late night snack. In the middle of the night when he felt a chill, he found his way to the basement and stoked the coal furnace. Hours after settling in, he strutted through the house, shirtless – kibitzing with Mama and Shirley – maybe this room rental thing wasn't so bad after all.

Two weeks passed. One afternoon Nick and Lee returned home from a day in the country; she carried a large straw basket covered with a pink blanket.

"This is little, Susie, our daughter," Lee said.

The beautiful blond, blue-eyed bundle was three months old and had been living with Lee's Mom in Utica, NY.

"Would it be OK if she stays in our room with us?" Lee made a request no one could refuse.

"No problem," Mama said, "how could I say no to this adorable little girl."

A few months went by and Lee sheepishly approached Mama again.

"I have a three-year-old son Johnny, from a prior marriage; he lives in Alabama with my ex-husband who is remarrying. Would you mind if he lived here with us?

"Of course not" Mama replied.

Benny's room was much too small for this burgeoning clan. So we switched; they moved into the master bedroom with its little annex. Shirley and I relocated to the back room, and Mom and Dad slept in the living room on the antique love seat and a folding bed.

Urine-soaked, soiled diapers, thrown into storage containers for diaper service pick-up, grew more and more pungent as the days passed, creating a stench that was well beyond the pale. Little Johnny loved running up the stairs and sliding down the banister.

Mama and Daddy enjoyed the kids and Nick's antics, but they longed for the day the Nicklesbergs would find more appropriate housing.

Then came the coup de grace; Lee's fifteen-year-old son Billy had been living down south with his dad too. Again, Mom agreed to Billy's migration north, but less enthusiastically. By this time, she began feeling sickly; she attributed her malaise to the reeking diaper pail, her constantly aching back from sleeping on a loveseat barely large enough to seat two, and her nervous state from the general chaos of nine people now living in a three bedroom house with a single bathroom sans shower.

After six months, Nick came home one evening all excited:

"Guess what?" he exclaimed, "Uncle Sam is finally coming through for us vets. We're moving into our own place in Mineola, Long Island."

"When," Dad asked unable to hide his own exhilaration.

"They just started putting up Quonset huts; they go up real quick and we're among the first to get in."

These inexpensive prefabricated, lightweight portable structures were built for wartime housing in the field but in 1946 the huge number of returning veterans unable to find affordable houses were happy to call them home.

Tears flowed as our extended family packed their belongings in the car trunk and on the roof, two boys in the back and little Susie on Lee's lap and drove off to their new home. Soon after they settled in we visited them. The Quonset hut was made of a row of semi-circular steel ribs covered with corrugated sheet metal with a plywood floor. It's 720 square feet of usable space was a big improvement over the room they had at our house.

Mama quickly painted, disinfected the furniture and bedding, and soon the diaper odor was gone. Mama, Daddy and I moved back into the master bedroom and Shirley returned to the "little room." with its single bed and skirted dressing table.

Ah, we had our home back.

Not so fast. There were three more years of tuition to be paid.

A carnival of strangers continued to occupy the back room and, to this day, my memory.

Mama spent hours consoling Mary, the next roomer, a 90lb, thirty-something woman to stop drinking and get rid of her companion Jim who was and always would be a drunken loser.

"Thank you, I know you're right," Mary sobbed as she left for the bar around the corner in search of her love.

We watched as they staggered back holding each other up-- Jim about 6'2" tall and weighing about 160 pounds draped over 5'2" Mary.

They stayed about a month and moved on.

The "Room to Let" sign went back in the window. In early March 1947 at about 9:00PM the bell rang. When Dad went to answer it a young man wearing white shorts and a polo shirt stood shivering, a large suitcase at his side, pointing to the sign. Vasco had somehow found his way to the Bronx after debarking from a plane from Brazil. He spoke Portuguese with a little English here and there. Shirley was sixteen and couldn't hide her excitement when she saw this guy with his beautiful brown eyes and a thick head of wavy dark brown hair framing perfectly sculptured features.

He adapted quickly, bought some winter clothing and settled in. After he lived with us for several months, one day he was pacing up and down the block.

Dad sat on the stoop watching; finally he asked:

"Vasco, what is the matter?"

"Vasco in love." was the quiet response.

To Dad's knowledge he wasn't seeing anyone so he surmised that this was Vasco's way of saying he was horny. Before we knew what was happening our handsome roomer started to date a young woman who lived across the street. She was short and buxom, hardly the type we would expect our dashing Vasco to go for. But soon they married and Vasco became our neighbor.

Next, two men who had just come here from some place in Europe took up residence in "the" room. We had some laughs at the expense of their language difficulties. Then there was Tom, the long-haul trucker, who regaled us with tales into the wee hours of the morning about his trip and exploits with the women he encountered at every port. After Tom moved on, a young woman who lived around the corner married; she and her husband rented the room for a few months until they were able to find an apartment.

So it went from September 1946 to June 1948, when the "Room to Let" sign was retired for good.

A distinguished looking gentleman, gray hair, six-feet tall, clad in a neat suit, wearing glasses, and carrying a stuffed briefcase along with a suitcase, rang the bell to inquire about renting the room. He explained that he was a writer and he certainly looked the part. He went on to say that he was working on a project involving a home for alcoholics several blocks from where we lived to complete research he was doing on alcoholism. For a few days he left in the morning and returned in the evening; unlike our earlier guests he was more of a loner.

After he was there two weeks, 4:00 o'clock one morning, the firemen came running into the house, yelling:

"Fire, Get out of the house! The House is on fire!"

"Where? Not our house!" Mama shouted back in disbelief.

"Yes YOUR House, get out now."

Mama and Daddy tried to wake me. I was nine years old and a very heavy sleeper. The firemen shooed them out, carried me, fast asleep, down the stairs and to the Fiskey's house and went to work putting the fire out.

The back of the house was completely destroyed as was the porch. One of the firemen approached Daddy and asked him why he had a mattress in the backyard:

"Mr. Beck, why is there a mattress up against the back outside wall?"

"There's no mattress there," Dad responded, having no idea what the fireman was talking about. When they went to the back, there it was, a burnt up mattress. The two went back up to the rented room where they realized that the roomer had been sleeping on the bed spring. He had obviously returned home late from his "research" project, probably a few sheets to the wind, went to bed with a cigarette. When the bed caught fire he threw the mattress out the window and went back to sleep on the spring.

I awoke next door where there was an almost party-like atmosphere as the Fiskeys made bowls of strong coffee and rolls, fresh from Shultey's bakery, slathered with butter. I had no idea what had happened. When they tried to tell me it was just incredible to me.

After we were allowed back into the house that evening, it reeked of smoke, a distinct odor that would last for months. We didn't see the roomer all day. That night we barricaded ourselves into the front rooms, put a dresser against one door and a chest against the other, and listened for the entrance door to open, unable to sleep.

He never came back. He just disappeared into the night, never to be seen or heard from again. He was the last of the parade of peculiar paying guests who occupied Benny's room while he studied animal husbandry in a calm pastoral rural area of Bucks County Pennsylvania.

Chapter 31
Provisions for Cold Winters

When the last of the fresh summer fruits showed up in the produce stores we knew it was time to put up the preserves.

Mama blanched peaches, plums, apricots, cherries, and tomatoes in black enameled pots. Water boiled in other vessels to sanitize mason jars, tops, and pink rubber gaskets; all four burners on the old gas stove were fully engaged in the operation.

The assembly line buzzed along. Mama and Daddy, like generations before them, carried on the tradition of canning our favorite summer goodies for the rest of the year when they were not in season.

After the preliminary steps were completed, Daddy took the sterilized jars out of the simmering water with a long tong. Mama put the blanched fruits into the jars and added the sweet cooking liquid, making sure the containers were filled to just the right level.

Next, Shirley and I helped to put the sanitized rubber gaskets in place. Together we closed the jars loosely. Mama and Daddy then placed them back into a big black enameled stockpot of boiling water, and let them cook for about an hour. When they were cool enough, Daddy carefully removed them from the pot, and placed them like soldiers standing in formation, a few inches apart on the towel-covered surfaces all over the basement.

As soon as they were cool to the touch Daddy stacked the colorful jars on shelves he had put up in every nook and cranny he could find in the cool dark basement. The average yield of seventy-five to one-hundred vacuum sealed jars of tasty deserts and snacks just barely lasted until new summer fruit arrived.

Canning is not a lost art; I came across an article about it recently complete with rules and procedures. It made me wonder where Mama and Daddy learned how to do this more than a half century ago. Current canning guidelines, indicated that handed-down recipes do not follow the most up-to-date specifications:

"If using such a recipe, be sure to follow modern recommendations for heat processing times and temperatures.

They go on to stress how important it is to maintain *exact* temperatures to avoid the growth of bacteria and other harmful microorganisms:

"Heat jars in a pot of simmering water (180 degrees) – keep lids hot until ready to use but DO NOT BOIL."

Upon reading this procedure, I wondered how our preserves didn't give us botulism, stomach poisoning, or some other painful digestive distress.

What the fruits of our little factory operation did give us was a year's worth of gastronomical delights – deserts and snacks along with sweet memories of a family bonding experience that remains with me to this day. The shared pleasure of the annual canning event in that old kitchen factory in our basement preserved the warm glow of summer throughout gray winter days and beyond.

Chapter 32
Daddy's Little Helper

Mama paced back and forth as Daddy scaled the wooden rungs; the ladder wobbled and creaked with each step. Our old rickety stepladder was wedged, at a thirty degree angle, between the second story floor and the top of the opposite wall. It leaned over the staircase, creating a 20-foot drop from its top to the floor below.

When he was close enough to the ceiling, Daddy reached up and slid the lid that covered the opening to the roof into a pocket to the left and pushed the outside cap up onto the roof. He proceeded to make several trips up and down, hauling a five-gallon can of tar, a roll of tarpaper, trowels, knives and paint thinner, all of which he placed on the roof through the opening before finally hoisting himself up.

"OK, it's your turn," he said and watched as I brought up the rear, carrying a hammer, screwdriver, and cleaning rags. He took the tools from me and pulled me up via the thirty-inch, square gateway to the sky. By this time Mama's blood pressure was through the roof too.

"Thank God," she sighed, "watch that she doesn't fall." she directed.

"Don't worry, I won't take my eyes off her," he shouted down, winking at me.

We were summoned to the roof by a stain in a ceiling or water dripping in an upstairs room. Once there we located the source of the problem – usually a rupture in a seam between tarpaper layers – fixed it with globs of gooky black tar and leveled it with a trowel. To prevent leaks, every few years, we ascended the ladder to inspect the roof for normal wear and tear, replaced worn tarpaper and resealed open joints.

Upon our descent from the roof, our faces, hands and clothing were black and shiny. We looked like a couple of prehistoric creatures that were buried in the La Brea Tar Pits in Los Angeles; the tacky black gunk stuck tenaciously to my long locks, as well as my father's bald head, hairy arms and under our fingernails.

Mom's revulsion at the sight of us was countered by a smile of relief when we touched down safely. The whole time we were cutting, tarring, and smoothing, she walked back and forth visualizing me falling thirty feet from the flat roof with no barriers to the street below.

Most of our jobs were less dangerous; some, however, more repulsive. For example when water backed up in a sink or the only toilet in the house, we often had a major clean-up as we plunged and snaked away offending clogs.

"Ugh! This is disgusting," I gasped, holding my nose.

"It's not that bad, we'll get it done," Daddy assured me.

From time to time I had to do the dirty deed because my little hands were better able to get into small or awkward spaces like under the trapdoor in the basement where clumps of hair, sludge or other objects obstructed the main waste line.

"Good girl. I really couldn't have done that one myself," he'd comment.

Few things pleased me more than helping Daddy with the myriad odd jobs required to keep the old house habitable. My long "Shirley Temple" curls were the only clue to my gender. Dirty dungarees that could stand on their own, a tomboy shirt, and worn sneakers adorned my small thin frame as I tagged along on his rounds.

On most of these occasions Mama muttered under her breath,

"Why don't you hire somebody to do that; she's not a plumber."

Only on very rare occasions did we have to resort to calling in professional tradesmen. Together, Daddy and I chopped wood, sawed logs, repaired furniture (not his best skill – he believed form followed function and it showed), replaced washers, bled radiators and replaced broken valves to eliminate rattles that sounded like a train coming through the house, especially in the silence of the night.

I kept him company while he enclosed the space under the porch to make the chicken coop in the middle of our urban neighborhood and later when he built a set of Adirondack furniture for the back porch.

Daddy was a resourceful, analytical problem-solver who often created his own "Rube Goldberg" tools and contraptions like the snow shovel on wooden tracks that I couldn't budge. That didn't stop me from tracking behind with a small shovel; he laughed when I kept lowering my body to get more leverage until I ended up inches from the ground.

"Stand up straight, you'll hurt your back," he'd chuckle, continuing:

"I'll finish this; you go in the house before your mother kills me for causing you to hurt yourself or catch cold."

When I became a "tween," a word that didn't exist then, the "yuck" factor ended our father-daughter handyman team. Tar under fingernails, in hair, and on clothes was no longer acceptable.

Today, however, I often surprise Arnie when I fix door hinges, small appliances and minor electrical or plumbing failures around the house.

Every now and then I sense Daddy beside me, only now he's the helper.

Chapter 33
Here Comes Santa – Not

Santa didn't stop at our house. No Santa. No Christmas tree. Not even a wreath on the door. Like most Jewish kids I felt left out and envious; just what I needed – another reason to feel inferior. I didn't take it personally, but I wished the man in the red suit would come down our chimney. I would have been happy to leave him cookies and milk in exchange for some brightly colored packages under the Christmas tree I so yearned for, strewn with bright lights and ornaments.

It was not to be; not at our house. We didn't even celebrate Chanukah, which under the best circumstances, could not compete with Christmas.

All was not lost, however. My friends, Sissy Kelly, Mable McGrath and Marion Klausz all let me help decorate their trees. In each case, a few weeks before Christmas the families gathered around the tree. The parents opened boxes full of Christmas stuff carefully wrapped and preserved from prior years. There were glass balls, figurines of Santa and snow covered houses, tangled strings of cone shaped green, red and yellow and blue lights, as well as an "angel" or "star" topper. They bought fresh boxes of candy canes, tinsel garlands and streamers along with sparkling angel hair each year.

Everyone dug in. The Dad untangled the lights and plugged them in; if the string did not light up it was because of one dead bulb. Locating the culprit was time consuming, but through years of experience along with lots of trial and error, the man of the house always succeeded and soon there would be light. After the lights were strung on the branches and the lady of the house carefully hung the delicate glass ornaments and family heirlooms, my friends and I placed the remaining ornaments, candy canes, garlands, streamers and angel hair. Finally Mr. Kelly set up the model electric train that ran around the base of the tree.

I could only imagine how excited my friends were on Christmas morning. One year I was at Lenny's house when his older brother Michael unveiled a new shiny red Schwinn bicycle. Lenny's mouth and eyes opened wide at the sight of this glistening conveyance. Michael, biceps bulging, carried the bike down the four flights of stairs to the street. Oblivious to the frigid temperatures, Lenny jumped on it and rode up and down the block, nose red, face frozen in an ear-to-ear grin.

The closest I came to Santa was at the age of twelve, a bit big to sit on his lap. Yet, that is what I did and I had a picture to prove it. He was especially nice to me because Shirley was his special helper.

For four years running she made sure she was available to work at McCreary's department store in Manhattan during the holiday season; she set up and sold photos of children sitting on Santa's lap. To her, there was nothing better than working with the out-of-work actors who played Santa and other staff who came back year after year.

Like everything else this annual tradition has changed since my childhood. Outdoor decorations that were relatively scarce and sparse have morphed into massive displays of lights on trees, shrubs and rooftops; humongous, sometimes garish, lighted blow-ups of Santa's sleigh and reindeer lie dormant on lawns by day, then inflate to illuminate the night sky.

Gift buying has become a commercial blockbuster with "Black Friday," "Cyber Monday," and "Green Monday," the last free shipping day before Christmas. Panic buying begins late on Thanksgiving night and goes into the wee hours of Friday morning; Shoppers stampede and trample each other to grab deals. Cyber Monday offers consumers another opportunity to be parted from their money via the internet. Most recently retail stores have begun to stay open all night on Christmas Eve.

If our forebears were able to witness this madness they would find it hard to believe. No doubt – affluence, colossal changes in communications as well as technology – have forever altered the way Christmas has and will be celebrated over the years. Still, to use the old cliché: "the more things change the more they stay the same."

Holiday music inundates the season on the airways, stores and public places;

I continue to sing and hum with it, albeit totally off-key. The air is filled with good cheer. It is, as always, a season when friends and strangers exchange pleasant greetings and families assemble to celebrate together.

Most important, while Santa does not come down my chimney, he continues to delight children of all ages with his red suit, white beard and hearty:

"Ho – Ho – Ho – Merry Christmas!"

Chapter 34
Goodbye to Teacher Who Turned the Tide

The crossroads of my life in June 1950 was bittersweet. I had overcome years of life-changing ups and downs and was about to move forward. The problem was that I had to leave Mrs. Timpson, the teacher who had transformed me.

I can still see her sitting on a stool in front of her desk — rarely did she sit behind it. Her light brown skin, small straight nose, wheat-colored stripe in her dark hair bore witness to her interracial heritage. The gold streak in back of her head was visible only when she freed her long, silky locks from their customary bun to brush them until they shone. When she smiled, tiny creases crinkled at the corners of her bespectacled, kind brown eyes.

Mrs. Timpson was warm, open and giving, not like the teachers I had before. I can't remember her scolding anyone, or putting a student down. She maintained complete control, yet let us know when we did something wrong; always in a constructive, encouraging manner.

I am forever grateful to Mrs. Flax for putting me in Mrs. Timpson's "Opportunity Class." Mrs. Flax was the first teacher to recognize my problem and do something about it by bringing Mrs. Timpson into my life. It was the best thing that could have happened.

She intuitively did the right thing for the twenty-five fifth graders who needed a little extra TLC. Each member of this not-so-elite group had an adjustment or learning problem: a bad stutter, a learning disability, hyperactivity, or like me, was extraordinarily quiet and withdrawn.

Mrs. T. geared everything toward making us feel good about ourselves. She was ahead of her time in understanding the importance of self-esteem and treating each child as an individual as well as instilling the importance of team spirit.

In between we studied the basic curriculum: math, reading, social studies, science, art, and music appreciation. Students who learned quickly tutored those who didn't, a system that helped both the tutor and the tutored. We didn't know what to do for her so we frequently invented reasons to chip in to buy her gifts.

It didn't take long before my stomach aches ceased. Not only did I talk, I also enthusiastically took part in class activities, tutored my classmates in arithmetic, took my turn as class President, and starred in class plays. I was back to being the average kid I was before I started kindergarten. By seventh grade, I and my fellow opportunity class alumni were mainstreamed and hadn't skipped a beat academically.

Years later, after I was successfully employed and attending college at night, I came across a newspaper article about a school in Harlem where reading and math scores had miraculously improved. The progress was credited to a new "Acting" Principal, who used unconventional methods to encourage kids to excel. She had instituted policies that celebrated success with frequent parties, encouraged teachers to use unorthodox activities to reward students, and established a more congenial atmosphere in the school.

You guessed it. Her name was Mrs. Timpson. She was now at the helm of what could have been referred to as the *"Opportunity School."*

I can only imagine how many lives, besides mine, this unforgettable educator and mentor transformed during her career; how many people she helped to enjoy richer, happier, more productive lives because she simply gave them the "opportunity."

Chapter 35
Coming of Age in the Fifties

Did we enjoy the fabulous forties – the big bands, Frank Sinatra and the 'bobby soxers?" How about the sixties when 70 million baby boomers became teenagers, college students rebelled, lived in communes, and attended a wild concert at Woodstock?

Those of us who came of age in the fifties were sandwiched between the excitement of the forties and sixties. Between 1951 and 1960, I went from eleven to the ripe old of twenty-one, the age of consent.

The world had for the most part recovered from World War II but with all the celebrations we weren't at peace for long. The Cold War between the United States and the Soviet Union was going into high gear. It set the stage for the Korean War and later the Vietnam War.

Following World War II the threat of nuclear war, the "Red Scare" touched us most directly when we had to hide under our desks. The bell rang and we were either ushered to a safe place in the school building or we dropped to our knees, crawled under the desk, bent forward and covered our heads. When I was in seventh grade we were issued dog tags just in case.

With all that was going on, perhaps one of the most important developments for those of us on the threshold of becoming teenagers was "rock-and-roll" becoming the new music craze. It knocked most of the "feel-good" post World War II pop songs off the charts with songs like "Rock Around the Clock" on juke boxes. Having missed the big band era of the forties, my friends and I were still listening to and singing along, with the help of song sheets, to the tunes of Perry Como, Nat King Cole and Frank Sinatra. The new sound was a welcome revelation to us. It sparked the beginning of the "generation gap," that really took hold in the 1960's.

The 50's are also known as the golden age of television. Popular sitcoms – "I love Lucy,' 'Father Knows Best,' and 'Our Miss Brooks" – filled our leisure time. We were among the last to have a TV so I went to other people's houses to watch these along with classics like Milton Berle's "Texaco Comedy Hour' on Tuesday nights and the 'The Ed Sullivan Show' every Sunday. That was better than standing and watching TV in front of an appliance store – as many did.

We were accustomed to being last to acquire any new device; we used the telephone in the candy store or the building across the street to make or receive an occasional call.

In the early 1950s, however, it looked like things might be shaping up for the Beck family. I graduated from elementary school in 1950 and started seventh grade back at P.S. 6, where I had been perhaps the only student to drop out of kindergarten six years earlier. It was the same year that Benny graduated from college and went to work on a farm in his beloved Bucks County, Pa.

A few years later Shirley returned home from a short hiatus. Mama was preoccupied with fears of Benny being drafted into the Korean War. In 1953 he was; Mama's fear of the military was realized. Benny was discharged soon after and married Doris.

About that time Dad had just gone into his own business with great expectations that unfortunately did not materialize.

In 1956 I completed high school and went into the workplace and contributed to the household somewhat easing the financial problems that caused much of the turbulence that had plagued us.

That same year Shirley married Gerry and set up housekeeping nearby.

By the end of the decade Ned, Neil and Brad had become the first of the new generation of decedents to come into the world.

The Becks seemed on course to a better life.

Chapter 36
Dropout Returns to School of Discontent

In September of 1950, older, wiser and more self assured, my return to PS 6 for the second time was a far cry from my half-day there as a green kindergarten student. I had no choice; it was where I had to go to complete seventh and eighth grade, after which I would go to high school.

I was mainstreamed back into regular classes. Academically I hadn't skipped a beat despite the fact that Mrs. Timpson spent little time on that aspect of our education. I also did OK on the social front. Soon after I got the hang of changing classes for different subjects and observed the monitors in the halls, exits and stairwell landings I became a member of this elite team of watchers. Stationed at a heavily trafficked stairway landing, my job was to maintain order.

One day I heard loud, non-stop talking heading my way. Before long I saw the source – a girl, whose tough reputation preceded her, rounded the corner onto my staircase at the landing below. When she approached I put my finger to my lips:

"Shhh, be quiet," I said quietly.

"Make me," she snarled.

"Get out of that line and stand right here," I ordered, gently pulling her arm.

She remained by my side until every class completed its trek up the stairs. Then I wagged my finger, warned her to be quiet whenever she passed my post, and let her go without writing up a charge. I reserved written charges for offenses like pushing, threatening or outright fighting. Violators went before Mrs. Sweeney, our music teacher and supervisor of our small army of monitors who maintained order in common areas. She reprimanded offenders, gave them a few whacks with a paddle covered with years of student's carvings, and then invited them to add their initials for posterity.

"Don't you know that she carries a razor blade in her sock?" friends questioned after seeing my prisoner. "Are you crazy?"

No and yes; No, I did not know about the razor and yes, maybe I was slightly wacky. God knows I was an unlikely candidate for the job of monitor. I hadn't grown much in the few months since sixth grade graduation, was almost skeletal and despite my new-found self confidence still quite shy and retiring.

I never ran into my nemesis kindergarten teacher who drove me from the school after a single half day and I rather liked my teachers in 7th and 8th grade. I remember Mrs. Smith, the math teacher, a large woman in her fifties with gray hair, she dressed plainly and wore no make-up. When girls came into class with lipstick on she bellowed at them:

"Why are you wearing lipstick? You look fine without it. When you get to be my age and your lips start to turn blue, that's when you need lipstick"

Whenever I or someone around me hiccups, I still think about Mrs. Wolf, our science teacher's novel halting of an embarrassing hiccup attack. Not quite five feet tall, 90 pounds, with cotton white hair and playful eyes, Mrs. Wolf was well liked. One day, in the middle of her lesson, she abruptly turned toward a "hiccupper."

"Barbara, get up here right now," she said sternly. Barbara looked around, puzzled and cautiously walked to the front of the room.

"Face the class," Mrs. Wolf ordered, "now hiccup for us!" Barbara stood, red faced, but no matter how hard she tried she couldn't hiccup.

Then there was Mrs. O'Connell, who taught "Home Economics." If it wasn't for her, graduation would have been an all-boy event. Making our own graduation dresses was the project for this segment of the sewing component of this course which was compulsory for all girls. To add insult to injury we had to wear the end results to graduation; no store bought dresses were allowed.

Mrs. O'Connell gave us a list of patterns to choose from and throughout the semester taught us how to pin the pattern to the fabric, cut the components, baste them together and use a sewing machine to complete the project, except for the hem which we had to do by hand.

Thankfully Shirley was an excellent seamstress. She walked me through the entire process, completing some of the steps for me. Since we didn't have a sewing machine at home, however, I had to finish the final sewing at school under the direct supervision of Mrs. O'Connell.

As we approached graduation day, like most of my female classmates, my biggest fear was that my dress would almost certainly fall apart and drop to my ankles in the middle of the days activities. Sewing was definitely not one of my fortes.

Truth be told that was one time I secretly wished I was a boy; was Freud right about penis envy? I don't recall his reasoning, but the truth is that life always seemed easier for them. This was just one example.

While we girls were forced to take "home economics" our male counterparts took "shop." We cooked hard boiled eggs, omelets, and French toast – all of which we had to eat. If that wasn't bad enough, we then had to clean the kitchen including all appliances; I always seemed to have to scrub the never-used toilet, bathtub and sink and remake hospital corners on sheets on the never-slept-in bed in our mock apartment.

Meanwhile the guys took a year to make a wooden lamp, bookends or a book-shelf. I would have much preferred that especially based on my experience helping Daddy around the house.

While we were forced to eat our projects and repeat the thankless job of house cleaning, they brought their projects home. And, no matter how they came out, their proud mothers prominently displayed their works of art in the living room.

As for the girl's pièces de résistance, not one dress disintegrated during the proceeding; after a long arduous journey, Mama, my dress and I all made it through the day.

It was time to move on to the hallowed halls of higher education. In my case, come September 1952 this one-time dropout would drop in at Theodore Roosevelt High School.

Chapter 37
The Prodigal Daughter Returns

Somewhat humbled by her short lived marriage experience, Shirley came home. Billy remained the persistent pest for a while; he continued to come to the house and cause havoc – to make us the spectacles of the block. What else was new?

In an effort to discourage his visits and because her nerves were frayed, Shirley left home again, this time for a few weeks in Pennsylvania where she spent time with Benny and Doris, his girlfriend at the time. When she returned she obtained an annulment and tried to resume a normal life.

She started a job that she actually liked. IBM had recently introduced mainframe computers; room-size machines that revolutionized data management. Shirley was one of the first "key-punch operators." The new concept intrigued her; she soon mastered it and quickly worked her way up through the ranks from operator to verifier to supervisor. She liked her coworkers and admired her supervisors who made these big machines do what they wanted them to through intricate programming techniques.

The job paid better than previous ones and she contributed generously to the household. An excellent shopper she bought nice clothing inexpensively, mainly at Klein's on 14th Street in Manhattan and Alexander's on Fordham Road in the Bronx, two popular discount stores. When she went to work in the morning it was as if she walked out of the pages of Vogue Magazine.

She also bought clothing for Mom and me as well as gifts like a Minnie Mouse watch, a birthstone ring and a brownie camera.

It wasn't long before Walter came into her life. He lived across the street and supported his widowed mother and younger brother. Walter was a travelling salesman, crisscrossing the country servicing retailers with a line of expensive curtains.

Shirley anxiously waited for him to come home from the road. She became a home-body; after work she spent her time reading "True Romance," sewing and making realistic looking crepe-paper flowers. Mama marveled:

"She has hands of gold; whatever her eyes see she can make." She seemed content for perhaps the first time in her life.

It wasn't to last. When his brother turned eighteen, Walter was drafted into the army. After basic training he was stationed in Germany. Shirley wrote him every night; she missed him very much. One day she came across some fabric that she decided would make ideal shirts for him; a perfect winter-weight, 100% wool, with a tiny checkered pattern in black and white and brown and white. She worked tirelessly, night after night, carefully hand-sewing, each stitch flawlessly consistent with the one before it, especially where they were visible on the yolks, collars and pockets. She couldn't wait for the day she would present the shirts to him.

Unbeknownst to her he had met a girl and fallen in love in Germany. Aware of how hurt she would be, he didn't tell her until he returned home while he was waiting for his fiancé's arrival after which they planned a small wedding. The news was devastating. Shirley's life began to unravel.

At about the same time she received news that her salary was going to be garnisheed. Dad's business wasn't doing well; he hadn't been making payments on the loan she cosigned for him. Subsequently she lost her job. It was hard to find a company that wanted to deal with the red tape of a garnishee. She worked on and off. During the off times household finances were worse than ever. Shirley responded by making some bad choices in relationships.

Then, in early 1956 she started dating Gerry, another young man from the neighborhood.

Gerry Sherman had recently returned from the army where he was a medic. At 6'4" tall, with wavy hair and horn-rimmed glasses, dressed to the teeth, he was very attractive. He looked like a real professional — maybe a lawyer. He worked as a draftsman and took engineering courses at night.

They married in October 1956 and took a small apartment in the northeast Bronx.

By January 1958 Shirley gave birth to Neil. I was nineteen. I remember the day well. I went with Mama to see them in the hospital. On the way, she cautioned me:

"Now remember no matter what he looks like, even if he is ugly, you say he is beautiful." He was pretty ugly; he looked like a little crimson, wrinkled old man. I of course admired and fell in love with him.

His was the first bris (ritual circumcision) I ever attended. I was his Godmother which theoretically meant that if anything happened to his parents, I and his Godfather – Gerry's brother, Irving would take care of him. In actuality, it meant we got to hold him during the ceremony. Dad had the honor of holding him while the Mohel (religious functionary who performs circumcisions) skillfully performed the procedure, a performance I managed to look away from as I heard him cry out. When I turned back to the procedure – Dad, his face now gray was being escorted outside for some air.

The young family soon moved back to our neighborhood, taking an apartment around the corner in the same building where Gerry grew up and his parents still lived.

By the end of the fifties things were looking up for Shirley and by extension those of us who loved her. We loved Gerry and took great pleasure in being part of the lives of Neil and Julie who was born two and a half years after her brother. I cherished being an aunt – even if I was referred to as Aunt Louie for a long time.

Chapter 38
Music to Mama's Ears Only

Violins screeched; trumpets squealed, and off-key piano notes reverberated throughout the building and onto the street below. The low-budget music school was above a dress shop on Tremont Avenue a few blocks west of Daly Avenue.

Mama was excited at the opportunity for me to learn how to play the piano at fifty-cents a lesson. Until then the most I did musically was sing from song sheets. I must say that when I sang with friends my voice always stood out — and not in a good way.

When I was twelve, Mama took me to meet with Miss Horowitz.

"We don't have a piano for her to practice on; is that okay?" Mama asked.

"No problem, our students come here to practice a few times a week. She'll do fine," Miss Horowitz assured her. Roz and I signed up.

The location in the midst of a busy shopping area was ideal. On our way to our lessons every Tuesday we stopped at Daitch Shopwell across the street. We picked sour-pickles from the large, brine-filled wooden barrel. With our lips amply puckered, we each bought a bag of greasy Cheetos. When our fingers were totally orange and oily enough to lubricate the piano keys we trudged up the narrow rickety wood stairway to a room that was barren, save for an old upright piano and a middle aged teacher waiting to make musicians of us.

Miss Horowitz hurried about on her three-inch, spiked heels; her fire-red, permed hair bobbed in and out of seven rooms to assess the progress of the world's future maestros. Her long eyelashes, thick with globs of black mascara, clown-like pink unblended circles on her cheeks, and ruby-red shiny lips, provided comic relief as well as an everlasting image.

Our training started with learning to read and write notes. Then we endlessly played scales. Next we moved on to melodies using the right hand notes only of "La Cucaracha," "Yankee Doodle," and "The Volga Boatman." Finally we learned chords for the left hand. When I had to combine both hands at the same time it was truly a case of the left hand not knowing what the right hand was doing. As for the foot pedal, I am still bewildered as to its function.

Regardless of my utter lack of musicality, Mama was convinced that my long thin fingers were meant to play piano. After several months of lessons, when a schoolmate's parents' were discarding her piano, Mama bought it so I could practice at home. It was a tall, ancient, battered upright – completely out of tune. Once Mama finally found someone to move it the few blocks to our house she had it placed in an honorary position in the corner of the living room. I set up my metronome, and arduously and repeatedly fingered the scales and assigned songs a few afternoons a week.

Subsequent to hearing me practice for a few weeks I think Mama began to accept that I would never become a virtuoso but she wasn't ready to give up. Convinced that it was teaching incompetence rather than my lack of talent that was keeping me from the concert circuit, she decided to give me private lessons with a young teacher who taught at his home. One of the first things he did was test my overall pitch perception and tonal memory. Not surprisingly he determined that I was, indeed, tone-deaf. Finally Mama gave up.

Notwithstanding this failure, I then went on to study the violin in high school achieving about the same level of accomplishment. It was more difficult because the notes are not as clearly defined as those on the piano. Nevertheless, I was in the school Orchestra as was everyone who took music. A second violinist, I was able to blend in relatively unnoticed. And, I got to enjoy the perks of legally cutting class to rehearse for weekly assemblies and special presentations.

In later life, I was surprised that I had not forgotten how to read music and was able to help my step-daughter Robin when she took on the challenge of the clarinet in her middle school orchestra.

To this day, whenever I have access to a piano, even a toy one, I play a respectable "Yankee Doodle" – right-hand melody only.

Chapter 39
Good Old Teddy Roosevelt High School

Stories of gang fights, stabbings and shootings at Theodore Roosevelt High School on Fordham Rd. filled newspapers and junior high school hallways throughout the borough. That was the school I was headed to after graduating from the last remaining elementary school in the system to go through eighth grade. That made us a year younger than most incoming students who graduated from ninth grade and the youngest of the entire student body. So it was with some trepidation that I entered this notorious establishment.

Despite its rough and tumble reputation, gang disputes usually stayed between rival gangs. They didn't bother students like my friends and me. Soon, using my well honed policing skills, I became a hall monitor again; this time my charges were bigger, more mature and tougher. I survived unscathed.

I also adjusted to the high school atmosphere. In the first two years I did pretty well academically, achieved good grades in math, language, science and especially English, always my favorite subject. Good grades entitled me to take honor classes in journalism and drama where I learned a little about newspaper writing as well as playwriting.

One morning in English class, Mrs. Peterson passed a straw bonnet around the room, and said:

"When the hat comes to you, take one piece of paper. I want you read your sentence and start writing something—anything that comes into your head."

My sentence read "Agatha took the pie with its unmistakable bouquet of fresh apples from the oven."

This was my first introduction to a "writing prompt." My mind's eye quickly saw a robust black woman who looked like Aunt Jemima of pancake mix fame. She wore a white apron, a bandana around her head, and a big smile. Enter two young children, laughing, and embracing Agatha around her hips.

She responded with a big hug and promptly prepared their breakfast. Before I know it I had written the beginning of a complete one-act play.

Fast forward to today, writing prompts usually have little impact on me. I strain my brain and continue to stare at the white space. Frustration increases. *Why can't I think of anything to write; if I do finally come up with some lame idea, why does it ring so hollow, so trite?* I wonder. *Has my internal hard drive become so crammed full of trivia over the years that it cannot conjure up an original idea?*

While I'm sure my Agatha play was not particularly creative it gave me great satisfaction to turn a simple sentence into a cohesive piece of work. I'm quite sure it influenced my feelings about writing.

Whether for my vocation, avocation, memoir, or simply to vent into a sporadic tome I loosely refer to as a journal, writing is something that consumes me and carries me far from everyday cares.

Writing prompts still inevitably evoke fond recollections of Mrs. Peterson walking around the halls of Theodore Roosevelt High School in her beige suit, white laced-gum-soled shoes, and short, soft, silver ringlets framing a smooth, jovial face. I see her stroll around the room to teach us the basic tenets of creative writing.

She was a living example of how keen teaching skills coupled with innate kindness, and encouraging words brought out the best in us. Moreover, she gave me a sense of self-assurance in a craft that allows me to escape into my own world . . . and lasts a lifetime.

A student, however, cannot live by liberal arts alone. My next favorite subjects were lunch and Phys. Ed. Still shorter than most of my classmates I loved basketball and volley ball. Supposedly we had to learn to swim in order to graduate but the best I could do was float face down and on my back, which is pretty much all I can still manage.

After a good workout I, the world's worst eater, pigged out at lunch; when I think back I can't imagine how I ate so much of that slop. Meat loaf, mashed potatoes and vegetables all drowned in brown gravy, followed by a piece of cake and a container of milk along with a candy bar for later. The activity and excessive eating must have balanced each other out because while I grew a few inches I remained quite thin.

Though I was enrolled in an academic program designed to go on to college, early on I knew that continuing my education would probably not be in the cards for financial reasons; so to hedge my bets I also fit a few commercial courses including steno and typing into my program.

As the subject matter became more difficult my grades were a bit less stellar but still respectable. I couldn't wait to go to work, contribute to the household and not have to remain dependent on Shirley to help make ends meet.

By the end of my junior year I had acquired enough extra credits to graduate six months early by taking two classes in summer school. January graduates did not enjoy the warm and fuzzy pomp and ceremony associated with June graduation; we just didn't come back for the spring semester. My last day of high school was January 27, 1956.

Chapter 40
Pondering Pop's Pompoms

The late afternoon sun poured through a wall of tall casement windows that rose to almost the full fifteen-foot ceiling, its cone shaped rays visibly capturing millions of flying white and pastel rabbit hairs.

I was fourteen when Daddy took the pompom plunge. During the 1950's, roller skates, ice skates, hats, and toys were adorned with pompoms. After years of working as a furrier, Dad decided he had the expertise to go into the business of making them. Besides having the requisite experience, it was feasible for him to borrow the small amount of start-up capital.

All of his life, Dad had been the antithesis of an entrepreneur. Even when he worked twelve-to-fourteen hour days, he was never quite able to make an adequate living. Many furriers, particularly those who worked in expensive lines such as Mink, Sable, or Beaver, earned very respectable incomes, while those who toiled in low-priced goods barely made a living wage. Daddy, unfortunately, was a sewing machine operator and some-time cutter of Mouton coats. Mouton is sheepskin sheered and processed to look like Beaver or seal, two more luxurious furs. At a fraction of the cost of high-end furs, Mouton was attractive, very warm, but extremely heavy, which may be one reason that it fell out of favor years ago.

I was the first and *only* kid on the block to have a fur coat when I was about eight years old. It raised some eyebrows in the neighborhood, particularly when I wore it to go trick-or-treating one year. When I was in my early teens Dad made matching, navy blue waist-length (Eisenhower) jackets for Shirley and me. He also made me another full length coat when I was about eighteen which he later converted to a ski jacket that I recently discarded not only because it would never fit me again, but I no longer have the strength to carry it.

Be that as it may, in the spring of 1953 Daddy acquired a $5,000.00 bank loan for which Shirley co-signed. He rented a loft in an old factory building on West Twenty-Seventh Street in Manhattan, bought a few used sewing machines, a minimum order of rabbit skins as well as some tools and supplies, and set-up his pompom business.

The shop measured about 30' x 30'. Two counter height, multi function tables served as cutting, counting, and packing surfaces. There were three sewing machines with accompanying old wooden chairs and a office. A dark, dingy, creaky, hand operated, self service elevator carried no more than four people at a time to the third floor enterprise.

Mama went in during the first week to try to help Dad. That didn't work out; she couldn't abide what she perceived as Dad not having the faintest idea of what he was doing. She couldn't help but compare him to her entrepreneurial father; with little hope for success she decided it was best to stay away.

Dad had no problem at the production end. The soft white, pink and blue fuzzy adornments were made from dyed rabbit skins cut into two-to-three inch circles. The operator loosely sewed a drawstring around the perimeter. The center of each circle was filled with cotton and the drawstring was tightly pulled and tied.

This venture provided me with summer employment for two years running. Every morning I took the hour ride on the subway from the Bronx to Manhattan. Once there, I stuffed pompoms, tried unsuccessfully to operate the sewing machine, helped with paperwork, held the fort when Daddy went out and made deliveries—always within walking distance in the fur district between Seventh and Eighth Avenues from about Twenty-Third to Thirty-Second Street.

The rest of the year there was always at least one employee. If there was a big order to get out Dad brought the supplies home and he, Mama and I sat around the dining room table, filled the pompoms, and pulled the drawstrings until our fingers bled. The room, our clothing, nostrils, and mouths were covered with fur.

When he saw my bloody fingers, Dad determined there had to be a better way to close the product and he set about finding it. Being somewhat of an inventor, he carefully examined the sewing machine operation. One pedal on the machine opened two jaw-like flanges allowing for the material to be inserted for stitching. He reconfigured it using two pieces of wood and rigged them to one of the sewing machines so that when you stepped on that pedal, the wooden blocks separated to permit the placement of the draw-string between them; another pedal closed them locking the inserted string and holding it tightly so that the operator pulled the soft pompom rather than the coarse string. Not only did this stop the bleeding it also decreased production time and increased productivity dramatically.

Mama was so proud. She thought her life partner had finally reached his potential; this invention would surely make him the world's prime pompom producer, purging the street of competition. It didn't take long, however, before Dad retrofitted at least one sewing machine for every other pompom maker in the fur district, thereby forfeiting his new found competitive edge. When Mama found out and chastised him, he angrily responded, disturbed by her lack of understanding,

"I can't make all of the pompoms!"

Just about ten years after it opened Dad's shop closed. With his heart failing he could no longer run it. A good friend helped me pack a few of his personal belongings, sweep away the final evidence of his labored presence, and lock the door on Dad's small furry final hope .

Chapter 41
All Gangs are Not Created Equal

It was a fall night, two girlfriends and I stole away to an area a half dozen blocks from home.

"What are you doin' around here?" came a voice in the distance.

"Just taking a walk," I shot back in the dark.

"Put that cigarette out," came the command, now a nose length away.

"Says who?" The words tumbled from my lips.

"Me — put it out or I'll beat the shit out-a-ya,"

The cigarettes that made us perfect prey were swiped from Shirley and Roz's mother. The street was deserted. Only the lighted tips of our cigarettes were visible.

The next thing I knew I was slammed against a parked car; a girl a little shorter than I had her arm across my neck and a group of about thirty teenagers chanted: "Go Lucy."

Splayed against the car, I quickly felt the smart of a hand across my face. My head jerked in the opposite direction. I heard chants:

"Go Lucy, hit 'er, again! LUCY! - LUCY! - LUCY!"

Lucy was a member of a group of teenagers who fancied themselves as tough guys and girls who, among other things, picked fights as a form of mischievous entertainment. Hers was one of many such neighborhood gangs who banded together to be "cool," cause trouble and most important feel like they belonged to something. Their method of operation was to assign one member the role of leader for the night and it was that person's job to start an altercation.

My adversary stood over me, all 4 feet, 10 inches and eighty five pounds of her.

"Keep it up Luce," the crowd goaded. Another smack, this time with the back of her hand, sent my head the other way. One slap followed another, my head swung from side to side in sync with each blow. The shouting continued:

"C'mon Luce, get 'er, get 'er good."

Several girls held Roz and Brenda motionless.

Lucy whacked my face from side to side like it belonged to a rag doll; she met absolutely no resistance. Was it shock? Perhaps it was because it was my first (and only) street fight? Maybe, if I remembered what Benny taught me when I was five or six, I might have at least tried to defend myself. The problem was we shadow-boxed and neither of us actually ever followed through with a punch; I don't know if I would have laid a hand on my opponent but I might have slowed her down.

Lucy's gang was relatively benign compared to the notorious gangs in our community as well as most inner-city areas across the country at the time. We often heard whispers of rumbles between the "Fordham Daggers" and the "Young Sinners," two of the most infamous local gangs. At one point rumors that the Fordham Baldies were coming to brawl with students from the studious Bronx High School of Science and the more macho, all-male Dewitt Clinton High School brought police and long traffic disruptions to the Mosholu Park area.

The Baldies, named after the Bald Eagle, according to a book and movie entitled "The Wanderers," supposedly shaved the heads and other body parts of opponents they caught. The Fordham Baldies I knew, many of whom attended Theodore Roosevelt, dressed in dungarees, black leather jackets, wore their hair in a Duck's Ass (D.A.) a hairstyle made famous by Fonzie in "Happy Days" and were feared by other gangs.

After a few minutes of pummeling, I felt something wet on my upper lip. My head was filled with cotton. Lucy stopped. She shouted:

"Get some water, tissues. Her nose is bleeding!" She anxiously blotted my nose, asking over and over:

"Are you OK?"

Still stunned, I nodded yes. Lucy and her cohorts walked away, the exhilaration of this night's mission a bit blunted.

Certain that by now Mama was out looking for me, we ducked into a nearby schoolyard to avoid her. Out of nowhere a pair of headlights came toward us.

Oh no, what now? Butterflies fluttered in my stomach; my heart pounded, my body tensed.

As the vehicle came closer we were at once relieved and scared to see a police car.

"Is everything alright, what are you doing in here?" the policeman asked.

Brenda quickly explained that we were on our way home from an evening walk.

The policeman looked at me:

"Did somebody hit you?"

"No, I fell," I murmured. "Yeah, she tripped" Brenda confirmed.

"You girls should not be here at night," the policeman scolded, "We'll follow you out. Make sure you go straight home before you really get hurt."

Whew, what a relief; I had imagined the police taking me home and Mama having an instant heart attack – or at the very least delivering a tongue lashing that would far exceed the sting of Lucy's hand.

We managed to make it undetected to Brenda's apartment around the corner from my house. We checked me over; there were no visible signs of my encounter. We scrubbed the blood off my "Theodore Roosevelt" sweatshirt and I went home.

Mama was both happy and angry to see me. She questioned where I had been so late. I muttered something that seemed to satisfy her.

She could never imagine what happened. I was the last person in the world one would expect to have an encounter with a gang. I was small, scrawny and scared to break the rules – friends often referred to me as a "Miss goody-goody:" I wouldn't participate in things like hitch-hiking, a practice that while common, was also dangerous and against the law; nor would I take a little something at the five and dime and not pay for it, or wear lipstick in school when it was forbidden. I certainly would never consider voluntary interaction with a gang.

The majority of boys didn't belong to gangs either but they were often tapped for protection money. A boy walking alone would likely be accosted by a wise guy, with:

"Give me your lunch money and you won't get the shit kicked out of you!"

A girl gang-member sometimes threatened less timid non-member under the guise of finding out the would-be victim was trying to steal her boyfriend's affections.

For days after my beating my head hurt almost constantly. I became nervous about it and told Mama about the incident.

"Why were you walking there at night?"

"To smoke," I responded.

"If you're so dumb to go into strange neighborhoods at night to smoke — if it's so important, smoke here," she blurted.

Eventually the headaches subsided. Unfortunately, however, the smoking accelerated.

A week later, at school, someone tapped me on the shoulder from behind. I turned around and there she was with a big friendly smile on her face.

"Hi," I'm Lucy, remember me? How's your nose? I'm sorry about the other night. I was gang leader for the night so I had to start the fight with you," she apologized. "Wanna hang out some time?"

Chapter 42
Korean Conflict Hits Home

The Korean War began when North Korea attacked South Korea in June, 1950. Driven by an almost manic fear of communism spreading throughout the world, the United States and many allies rushed in to defend freedom and democracy.

Though the fighting was taking place 6,000 miles from our shores it had a tremendous impact on life here. For one thing the draft, which had been eliminated after World War II, was reinstated. In our house that meant there was a good chance Benny would be drafted.

When he graduated from college and secured a job as a manager of a large dairy farm he received an essential occupation exemption, allowing Mama to breathe a sigh of relief.

The farm he ran was located in Morristown in Bucks County, Pennsylvania near his alma mater. It was owned by a prominent attorney, turned gentleman farmer. Benny was happy to be in the environment he loved; he liked the job, his boss and it seemed, the "farmer's daughter" as evidenced by several photos he took of her.

We didn't know what was actually going on in his personal life. He was not one to write letters or talk about his comings and goings. We would learn later that he had in fact met a girl at a social event that he attended with a friend from school. They became acquainted with two sisters, Doris and Marie Jones. His friend, whose name escapes me, was enamored by Marie as Benny was with Doris. They courted for some time before he brought her home to introduce her to the family.

She looked like a deer caught in headlights – coming into a New York neighborhood and meeting Mama with her Yiddish accent. Having grown up in a coal mining town in Pennsylvania, I believe the eldest of some seven children, she obviously experienced culture shock. Add to this the feeling of being put under a microscope by the family of your intended. She was quiet; who wouldn't be under the circumstances? In our future contacts, however, it seemed that she was generally a woman of few words.

We too were taken aback a bit when we first saw her. She wore a navy blue tailored suit, had straight shoulder length chestnut hair and brown eyes. She stood tall at about 5'11" just a little taller than Benny. All-in-all the visit went relatively well.

Soon after the family get-together, Benny's boss suddenly passed away. The executor of his estate quickly sold off the live stock making Benny's job obsolete. By now his relationship with Doris was rather serious; she didn't share his passion for farm management and given the demanding hours and responsibility it was understandable.

Benny took a job as a milk inspector with the USDA. This set him up for the loss of his deferment. Late in 1952 he received his "Greetings" letter from Uncle Sam. He came to New York, went down to Whitehall Street in Manhattan, passed his physical, was drafted into the Marines and sent to Paris Island, South Carolina for basic training.

Mama was a basket case — her worst fears became a reality. Paris Island had a reputation as one of the toughest training bases — they made the newspapers for abusing recruits; taking them on dangerous training exercises where some perished.

Within weeks we received notification that Benny had been hospitalized and was about to be transferred to a VA hospital in Pennsylvania.

The first weekend after his transfer Daddy boarded a bus at the Port Authority to visit. He learned that Benny had suffered a mental collapse and was diagnosed with Paranoid Schizophrenia — he was experiencing hallucinations, delusions and rapid mood swings. The doctors painted a dismal picture. Every Sunday morning Daddy took the train to the Port Authority terminal and boarded that same bus. Mama and I anxiously waited at the train station in the evening to find out if there was any improvement only to share Dad's disappointment. Shirley visited him a few times. Mama couldn't bring herself to see her Benny that way and at fourteen nobody wanted to take me along.

The wear and tear on Daddy was obvious; on some visits he witnessed alarming symptoms and watched as attendants took Benny away from him. The condition was aggressively treated with medications, therapy and electroshock sessions. After several months the old Benny began to slowly re-emerge.

The war that was raging within Benny's brain seemed to end as quickly as it had begun just months after the July 27, 1953 signing of the Peace Treaty at Panmunjom. Benny was discharged from the hospital, and soon after from the Marines.

The whole experience seemed surreal. The diagnosis did not make sense. Though he exhibited symptoms consistent with the disease, his recovery was inconsistent with lifelong implications of it. The patient blended back into society without ongoing care or medications and lived a relatively normal life

It's still a mystery to me. There are studies that link severe stress to similar symptoms which may occur in response to significant stressors in a person's life. In "Brief Psychotic Disorder," for example, the symptoms usually last for a shorter period but they end in eventual return to baseline functioning.

There have also been exposes about experimentation with drugs such as LSD on military personnel at that time. Shirley was convinced that was the case here. Whatever it was, the speed with which it resolved itself, absence of reoccurrence and Benny's ability to function are not consistent with the original diagnosis. And, we thank the powers that be for that.

In the fall of 1953 Ben and Doris were married. Communications between them and us continued to be sparse, only taking place when Mama, Shirley or I called them. They did let us know when Ned was born in 1957; they sent baby photos of the new addition and then from time to time followed up with more pictures of him playing in a cardboard box, on a swing or in his Dad's arms. Brad followed about a year later. Ross and Lynn joined them in 1961 and New Years Eve 1965 respectively.

Through the years Ben worked at a variety of jobs. At one point he worked for an artificial insemination company. It was his job to educate dairy farmers about the benefits of artificial insemination over natural reproduction methods and to perform the procedure on their cows.

In real estate, an accepted rule of thumb is that the three most important components in choosing a piece of real estate are location, location, location. This also holds true in other areas such as retail locations and in this case "AI." Ben was definitely in the wrong place. He tried his hand at this profession in, of all places Lancaster, Pa., home of the Pennsylvania Dutch. Though their farmlands are among the most productive in the nation, this is an old order of Amish and Mennonites, also known as "Plain People.' As the name implies, they use simple, old-fashioned, sustainable farming methods and live and work like their forefathers did.

It is easy to see why Artificial Insemination might be a hard sell in this community and why Ben had to move on to other ways to earn a living, which he did, ultimately becoming a Kirby Vacuum Cleaner distributor.

After operating the distributorship in York Pennsylvania for many years, his territory was folded into a neighboring one and he found himself out of business as he approached retirement age.

Ben went on to fight many battles from which there were no exemptions. He suffered several health issues including diabetes, heart problems for which he underwent open heart surgery, and finally cancer of the bladder to which he succumbed in 2004, months after his seventy-fifth birthday.

In an ironic twist, Doris who had a history of high blood pressure passed away in her sleep three short months later.

Whenever I called or visited Ben in his later years, he remained upbeat. When I asked:

"How are you?"

He always responded with a smile that I could even sense over the phone: "Still handsome."

Chapter 43
Cold Introduction to World of Commerce

One week after graduation and just one month shy of my seventeenth birthday, I stood on the frigid crossroad of the world, 42nd Street and Broadway, with the New York Times open wide to the help wanted section. A middle aged, well-dressed man approached:

"Are you looking for a job young lady?" he asked. 'You see that building across the street' he pointed, 'the company in room 114 on the first floor is looking for help. Go there; I'm sure you will get a job."

"Oh thank you." I replied, anxious to get into someplace warm.

I navigated to the other side of Broadway, walked into a big old office building, and opened the door to a dark dreary office. Blinding gray smoke hung in the air. Four or five old men sat hunched over dusty desks piled high with paper, cigarettes dangling from their mouths. One approached me.

"Can I help you?"

"A man on the corner told me you need help." I said my voice barely over a whisper.

"That we do," he replied. "Tell me a little about yourself. Where do you live? Where did you go to school? What kind of job are you looking for?"

After I answered his questions he went on to explain that this was a factoring company where, for a fee, they bought up accounts receivables from companies that needed operating cash fast. "We're looking for a file clerk; you can start right away; we work 40 hours a week and the salary is $40.00."

I accepted and by 11:00 o'clock I was putting stacks of invoices in alphabetical order and wondering: *what have I done now?* It seemed like several hours had passed when the boss came over and announced:

"It's 12:00 o'clock. You can go to lunch now. Be back at 1:00 PM."

I grabbed my coat, ran out of the building to the first phone booth I saw and called home.

"What should I do" I stammered, almost in tears, "I took a terrible job. I'm out to lunch now but I don't know what to do!"

Without hesitation, Mama said:

"Don't be upset, just take the train and come home."

As I walked to the subway, I asked myself: *am I going to be workplace dropout too?*

Chapter 44
Ripley's Believe It or Not

Five Days after my first "one-hour" job, I almost started my "real" first job. To many, the word Ripley's conjures life-sized figures of legendary people, strange phenomena and countless curiosities found at "Ripley's Believe It or Not Odditoriums" around the world. In Times Square, for example, visitors view exhibits of a 3,200-pound meteor rite, the tooth of a mastodon (a species that has been extinct for more than 11,000 years), and a six-legged cow.

To me, it brings back instant images of Ripley Clothes, Inc., my first long-term employer. They manufactured a full line of men's clothing and operated a wholly owned chain of some fifty retail outlets nationwide. On Monday, February 6, 1956, I set out for day-one of what would turn out to be a circuitous forty-year career. A bit wobbly in my new high heels, I walked the five blocks to the West Farms station carrying a pocketbook, bagged lunch, and as directed at an interview a few days earlier, my high school diploma. My one-hour job experience the week before added to my anxiety for which, as it turned out, there was good cause.

No sooner did I begin my twenty minute hike from the subway station at 72nd Street and Broadway to West End Avenue and 64th Street did I realize I was missing my diploma. I stopped and looked around the immediate area. My chest tightened. I couldn't think. Tears started to well up and my brain spun: *Should I keep going? Should I turn back? What will I say when I get there? What will they say?* I tottered on.

"What happened?" asked Mr. Lumish, the Office Manager, shocked when he saw my red eyes and tear streaked face.

"I lost my diploma," I sobbed.

Relieved, he replied:

"Oh, don't worry about that. Sit down, relax."

When I calmed down a little, he continued:

"OK, now go home. Call the school; tell them what happened and they will send you a duplicate diploma. Then come back and we'll put you to work"

I trekked back to the subway; when I arrived at the point where I noticed that I didn't have the envelope, I slowed down and attempted to retrace my steps the rest of the way, my eyes to the ground. Nothing. I went to the downtown side of the tracks where I had gotten off the train, bent over the platform and searched for something, anything tan, perhaps shredded by a passing train. Again – nothing.

"Hey, you over there; step back, don't lean over the edge like that!"

I looked up to see an angry police officer approaching, admonishing:

"Don't you realize you could fall over and get hurt or be hit by a train? You see this yellow line? Never step over it again."

I tried to explain, but he wasn't moved by my loss and suggested I move along.

So for a second time in a week I came home from a work-related episode upset, dejected and thinking that maybe I made a mistake by pushing my graduation up; *could it be that I wasn't ready?*

"Don't worry," Mama held me. "Things happen, it will be alright."

I called the school and they told me that there was no such thing as a duplicate diploma. The best they could do was write a letter on school stationery confirming that I was, in fact, graduated on Friday, January 27, 1956. The letter would be ready in the afternoon if I wanted to pick it up, which I did.

The following morning I sheepishly returned to Ripley's and presented Mr. Lumish with proof of my graduation. He smiled, welcomed me and took me up to a tiny office on the fifth floor, adjacent to the factory. He introduced me to Mildred Hay, Director of Payroll, a big job for a woman who stood less than five feet tall, weighed about 85 pounds, in her early forties. I met two other young women whom I would join to complete the Payroll Department.

One was looking through a large stack of oversized printed sheets, perforated top and bottom attached accordion style. I quickly learned this was a computer run showing employee names, lot numbers and the number of garments per lot. Our job was to code piece-workers' job sheets, examine resulting computer runs for discrepancies between original lot-size and number of pieces reported by employees, investigate them and discuss the differences with the workers. Our findings often led to a reduction in an upcoming paycheck which was difficult for us as well as the affected person after he or she worked a forty-hour week, hunched over a sewing machine, standing at cutting table or sweating from the heat of a large press.

Mildred was congenial and fair, but a tough boss. She was also the first aid administrator extraordinaire. Most days one or more people sought her expertise to remove a particle that had flown into an eye, bandage a minor cut, or dole out aspirin for a splitting headache.

Once, two workers escorted a sewing machine operator into the office. His face ashen grey, eyes wide with fear, right hand holding its left counterpart. My eye caught sight of a needle clear through his index finger; I gasped, my face must have turned pure white as I let out an:

"Oh, my god!" and covered my eyes.

Mildred shot me a *look*, quickly turning to the injured man.

"That doesn't look so bad," she comforted him. "Just sit down here and we will get you to the hospital right away."

She sat with him until an ambulance came to escort him out. Then she turned to me:

"What is wrong with you? Didn't you see how frightened he was? Your response certainly didn't help! If you ever do anything like that again you are gone!"

Many years later, long after I had almost forgotten my legendary first day at Ripley's, I received a scuffed, dirty, brown envelope in the mail. The return address: New York Board of Education, Brooklyn, NY. Yes, it was my high school diploma – believe it or not.

Chapter 45
Anatomy of a Career-Setting the Course

"I'm rich!" I shouted flying through the door with my first paycheck. The thirty-three dollars and change after deductions created an exhilaration that I would never again experience, certainly in connection with money. That feeling was exceeded only by the realization that I was finally an independent adult playing a primary role in my own life.

That first real job as a payroll clerk offered a degree of autonomy and a measure of anonymity that allowed me to escape the constant scrutiny of management in the main office. Frequent jaunts in and out of the factory, back and forth to the computer department and to distribute paychecks throughout the building gave me an opportunity to meet and socialize with lots of people at all levels. I talked to them about what they did and found myself wanting to learn more.

My small income and the little Daddy drew from the business reduced financial anguish in a big way. Slowly we paid off back taxes and caught up with the mortgage. Hostilities cooled.

One night as we relaxed at home Dad began to violently and uncontrollably throw up. He had terrible pain in his abdomen, his hernia protruded and he was unable to push it into place. My friend Ann and I grabbed a taxi and took him to Fordham Hospital, one of several public hospitals throughout the city. The waiting room was mobbed. We checked in at the desk, took seats and waited. Daddy looked worse by the minute; from time to time I tried to reason with the personnel pointing out that this was a true emergency.

Finally his name was called. We waited for what seemed like hours until a doctor came to speak to us.

"Your Dad will be fine, he had a strangulated hernia which we were able to put back in place; we're going to keep him here overnight and he should be fine for now. But he has to have surgery soon because this will happen again and it could kill him. You can go see him in a few minutes."

About a half hour later we found him in a ward crowded with about twenty men. Dad smiled through tears of relief. His color was back. Words of praise for the two young doctors who treated him rushed from his mouth the minute he saw me:

"They saved my life! It was amazing. One held my shoulders, the other my feet. They picked me up and shook me until the hernia went back into place."

I was grateful but the realization of life without medical insurance literally hit home.

There are times when the Emergency Room is absolutely necessary but the waiting, callousness with which the personnel treated us and others, and then seeing all those patients stuffed into the ward like sardines upset me so that I vowed to somehow get medical insurance for Mom and Dad.

When I told Mildred about what happened she hugged me:

"I'm so sorry you had to go through that. We can help by putting your parents into our group policy." What a relief that was; another step in the right direction.

The slow but steady improvements in lifestyle made me want more. The opportunity to advance in the payroll department was little to none. So, as much as I loved Mildred, toward the end of the first year I managed to transfer to the bookkeeping department as an "accounts receivable" clerk.

It wasn't a big jump; rather one small step with a better chance to grow. The work was similar – only the faces and the documents changed – instead of job sheets, we coded store receipts for computer processing and reviewed the resulting IBM runs to ensure everything was entered accurately in the accounts receivable journal. We also completed forty or fifty monthly bank reconciliations, one for each store; to this day I dutifully reconcile the family check book every month.

In the large general office I interacted more with the Accounts Payable and Accounting departments. I started to learn something about bookkeeping and became aware that an assistant bookkeeper in a small to medium size firm was paid $60.00 to $70.00 a week and a good full-charge bookkeeper could gross close to $100.00 – I was earning $45.00. *Hmmm*, I thought, *I could do that.*

In September 1957, I registered for Accounting 101 and attended classes two nights a week. The first two "Accounting" courses at the downtown branch of City College of New York, now Baruch College, covered the entire bookkeeping process and I qualified for matriculation and free tuition by virtue of my high school average.. The following spring I followed up with Accounting 102.

Work and school would keep me busy for many years to come. In between I began to come into my own. I started to enjoy eating out and socializing with friends and seeing the latest Broadway hits, including many original musicals. The excitement of that first paycheck was making its way into other aspects of life.

Chapter 46
Ticket to Ride

Gas: thirty cents a gallon. Mode of transportation: '49 Nash in 1957. Total cost of an evening of recreation, discovery and amusement: one dollar.

"Wanna go for a ride?" Tiny asked, pulling up in his well-worn coach.

Roz, Sybil and I jumped in for a trip to City Island, Orchard Beach or through the Westchester countryside. With little to do and limited funds, driving around aimlessly was a common form of pastime. Although Tiny was the youngest of our small posse, his love of the automobile made him the first of us to own one.

I couldn't wait to drive. Soon after I turned eighteen I got my learner's permit and Tiny started teaching me. The stick shift required some fancy footwork between the clutch, the gas and the brake. If you let the clutch up too fast as you shifted into gear the car bucked – shook, rattled and jerked forward in short spurts, especially in first gear. I never quite mastered getting off to a smooth start. Nor was I able to surmount the other tricky maneuver of keeping the car from rolling backwards when starting uphill from a full stop; you had to release the clutch slowly with your left foot as you gradually fed the gas with your right foot; when you felt a slight pull, you released the hand break with your right hand and steered the car with your left. Easy – perhaps, if you're an octopus.

Tiny was a stickler about hand signals, even when there wasn't another car in site. For one thing, he didn't have mechanical ones or they didn't work; for another, proper use of hand signals accounted for a major part of the road test. It didn't hurt that every time I didn't put my hand out the window he got to smack my knee which remained black and blue for the duration of my driver's education. Most evenings he picked Roz, Sybil and me up, drove to a relatively isolated area, and gave us each a turn at the wheel.

If the Nash hadn't died when it did I may never have been able to drive. It was the automatic transmission in Tiny's next jalopy that made my learning possible. What a difference! Thanks to automation and my instructor's diligence I easily passed the driving part of the test. My hubris, however, did me in on the written segment. I was quite embarrassed when I went to the DMV to retake the written test and was the only English speaking person who had failed to respond correctly to the very simple series of questions that came directly from the handbook book that I never read.

Almost immediately after I received my license in 1958 I purchased a one-third share of a brown '52 Chevy convertible; my two partners were of course Roz and Sybil. Total cost: $250.00. Again, we imposed on Tiny to check the car out for us. He told us about the leaking transmission and a few other things, none of which deterred us.

The partnership worked since we were usually together anyway. The car, however, did not. Almost immediately, we felt the transmission slipping; we added transmission fluid and it leaked right out. I drove the car to work one morning and left it with the mechanic across the street from my office to see what he could do. His prognosis was bad: "Nothin' you can do except replace the transmission and that'll cost more than the car. I got this '51 Studebaker – runs real good. We can trade – even-swap."

This was an offer we couldn't refuse – how much worse could it be?

It didn't take long to find out. One day Roz pulled up in front of my house and double parked even though there was an empty spot right there.

"Park the car," I shouted, "I need a few minutes."

"No," she replied.

"Just park it," I insisted.

"No," she repeated quietly.

"What's wrong with you, just park the damn car!"

"I can't," she finally declared.

"Why not," I asked, quite agitated by now.

"It won't go backwards" she said with a smirk.

We continued to drive our newly acquired lemon forward – until all the gears went at which time we junked it.

I kept my eyes open for another car. This time I would buy it on my own with the IRS refund I expected any day. I saw a 1952 forest green Pontiac convertible parked in the corner of a gas station with a "For Sale" sign on it. I inquired about the price which was $250.00, the same as the Chevy and the amount of my anticipated refund check.

Thankfully, I had learned from my first experience. The first thing I did before making a deal was to look under the car. I saw a puddle of liquid and told the proprietor, "forget it; this car is leaking transmission oil."

"No it isn't," he replied looking me straight in the eye."

"What do you call that," I asked pointing to the black, viscous fluid.

"Oh that," he quickly explained, "up until a half-hour ago there was another car in that spot with an oil leak."

I anxiously checked the mailbox for my refund every day and periodically confirmed that the car was still there. It drove Mama crazy.

"Don't worry," she reassured me, "that bargain will wait for you. How can you be so dumb after what you just went through?"

"Anyone can make a mistake," I said, thinking *what does she know about cars?*

The minute I received my refund check I hitched a ride to the gas station and believe it or not my chariot awaited right where I had first laid eyes on it.

Of course, as Yogi Berra says, it was "déjà vu all over again." In no time I was once more without wheels.

Eventually, after several other used cars, the last of which was a dependable '65 Dodge Dart, I accompanied my friend Ann to several dealers. She had been searching for a new car for months and did her homework, settling on the 1974 Dodge Dart or Plymouth Duster, both highly rated for dependability. Arnie joined us to offer his "male" expertise and protect us from the big bad salesman who would undoubtedly take advantage of our gender-induced ignorance.

Sensing a complete lack of enthusiasm for what we saw, Arnie suggested:

"Why don't you look at the Chevy Camaro-it's a beauty?"

We drove up to the dealership and gasped in unison at the sight of the sleek gold car perfectly lit in the circular corner display-window. One quick, cursory look – no research, no test drive, no kicking the tires, checking the back seat or the miniscule trunk – Ann asked for the price. Before the salesman finished his response, she said:

"I'll take it."

I, who had no need, intention or funds to buy a new car followed with:

"Do you have two?" I had no idea where those words came from.

So, with the help of my friendly banker, I bought my first brand new car strictly on impulse. It felt good. Aside from slipping and sliding at the slightest sign of snow or ice, a near unusable back seat and an almost non-existent trunk, it turned out to be the dream car of my life that served me and my future family well for the next fifteen years.

Chapter 47
Dad's Cutting Triple Play

Dad had enjoyed relatively good health most of his life. In his mid-sixties, however, he was slammed with triple surgery that put him out of commission for almost six weeks. Although he had reached retirement age he was still very much into succeeding in his small business – in fact he *was* the business – without him it did not run. Toward the end of 1958, run Dad did – this time it was to the bathroom constantly. Like many men of a certain age, his prostate had become enlarged and caused this debilitating phenomenon.

On one occasion he experienced another common symptom of this condition; when he made it to a facility he was unable to complete his mission. Frightened, he rushed to the emergency room at the nearby French Hospital on West 30th Street and was told he needed surgery, pronto.

That would mean closing shop for a few weeks. He went back to the shop to begin to prepare for the inevitable. He completed his open orders and made arrangements for some of his friendly competitors to take care of his customers in his absence.

Day-by-day his condition worsened. Soon he had no choice but to check into the hospital. On the appointed day Gerry, who had just recently married Shirley, volunteered to drive him. For his kindness Dad took him on a wild goose chase:

"Before we go in could you please drive me to 28th Street; I have to drop a check off to my supplier."

No sooner did they restart their journey did Dad have to go to the bathroom.

"Pull over there" he said pointing to Bickford's where he would use their men's room. When he returned to the car Gerry asked:

"OK, Dad, Ready to go to the hospital now?"

"One more stop please; I must go to the shop for a minute."

Gerry dutifully drove him to 27th Street. The way Gerry told it, there were several more pit stops (Dad knew every public facility in the area) before they actually arrived at the hospital and checked in.

Built by a French society in the late 1920's and run by an order of kind caring nuns, the hospital went broke in the sixties and is now a high-rise condominium.

A doctor in his early thirties performed the initial exam; he found that Dad's prostate was enlarged consistent with a man of his age and needed to be taken care of. But what really took him aback were the two extremely large sacs that protruded from the lower abdomen.

"How long have you had those hernias?" he asked.

"I don't know – many years," Dad passively replied.

"Don't they bother you?"

"Sometimes, but I push them in when they're really bad. I wear a truss for a week or so and that helps. A few years ago one strangulated."

"Well, while we have you here I think we should take care of that too. We'll do all three surgeries, one week apart, and you'll feel like a new man."

Dad looked around at the six men in the ward who had undergone a prostate reduction procedure. Each had a bag of blood hanging from the side of his bed. They had all been hospitalized for more than a week and looked pretty bad for the wear.

The doctor went on to explain that rather than reducing the prostate he preferred to remove the gland completely. He told Dad that he had success with his method but that it carried serious potential risks including incontinence, impotence and nerve problems.

"If all goes well, however," he continued, "the recovery is faster, less painful and there are less negative side effects. It's up to you; I can do it either way."

"I'm in your hands," Dad replied, "do it your way."

The surgery went well. When the doctor came back for the post surgery exam, Dad thanked him profusely and kissed his hands:

"God bless those hands," he said with tears in his eyes. He had none of the possible devastating side effects.

After a few days of rest he was back in the Operating Room where other surgeons repaired his right rupture. While he was recuperating it was suggested that the left tear in his abdominal wall was so bad that even after it was closed, before long it would probably open again. One way to try to avoid that was to remove his left testicle.

That was the last straw – no way would he allow that.

"I'm leaving this world the way I came in. Forget about it."

The decision was made to go ahead with the third surgery as per Dad's wishes and hope for the best.

During the three weeks Dad was in the hospital his long-lost sisters Dora and Nettie showed up one day. They were the youngest of his siblings and were very close to each other all their lives. From early childhood the family referred to them as "the girls," an expression that is still loosely used among women of all ages.

The sisters each married late in life and neither had children. They spoke to each other almost daily and met for lunch in the city on a regular basis into their eighties when Dora moved to Florida.

Shirley had maintained limited contact with Dora throughout the years so she called her and told her about Dad. He had almost no personal contact with his sisters since the early forties. Their only communication since was at the funerals for Ida and Molly, both of whom had passed away a short time ago within two years of each other.

When Mom visited Dad a few days later she asked:

"So, did you have a nice visit with the girls?" He shot back:

"The Girls," how long will they be girls? They're old women already,"

Soon after he came home they came to see him once or twice before things went back to normal; contact was lost again.

Dad made a speedy recovery from his triple play surgery and picked up where he had left off. Before long he was back to working fifteen to sixteen hours a day, trying in vain to achieve some measure of success before it was too late.

Chapter 48
Full Charge Ahead

In late 1958, with all of six accounting credits under my belt and having completed a "practice set," a simulation of a complete set of books for a make-believe company, I thought surely I was ready to be a full-charge bookkeeper.

A nice young manufacturer of plastic bags used to cover freshly cleaned clothing, wrap packages, and other applications, agreed and hired me to keep his books. We were both wrong.

The factory was located on Brook Avenue in the South Bronx near the Willis Avenue Bridge, one of the poorest neighborhoods in the borough, probably the city. The area was dominated by a mixture of old rundown tenements and industrial buildings inhabited largely by unemployed men who spent their days on nearby stoops looking for trouble. Inside the plant, a strong chemical smell permeated the entire building. Except for short periods when the boss dropped by to place or check orders, I was alone in a tiny office.

At nineteen, coming from an environment where I enjoyed the camaraderie of some thirty co-workers, many my own age, with whom I shared daily lunches, cigarette breaks and lots of laughs the loneliness was tough to take.

The phone became my best buddy. Talking to old friends helped. One, Sybil, followed my lead and took a job a few blocks away. She occasionally visited and joined me for lunch at my desk. There was virtually no place to eat. On her last trip she arrived pale, visibly shaken, and crying, she managed to utter:

"I just got fired."

Just then, my boss came into the office; he was sympathetic to Sybil and assured her everything would be OK. She would get another job and put this behind her.

The following Friday morning he again came into the office. He told me what a good job I was doing and then continued with:

"Much as I regret it, I have to let you go. You're very young and I made a mistake by hiring you for this job. I know that you must be lonely and you spend lots of time talking to people outside the office. Everywhere I go in the plant I see the phone lit up. I don't mind, but it has a negative effect on the personnel. I am sorry but you may not be quite ready for a one-girl office."

I was dumbfounded. *How stupid can you be?* I chastised myself. *What were you thinking? Now what? Who's gonna hire you now?* For some time on the trip home I sobbed and berated myself for being so irresponsible. I could not afford to be out of work.

It took months before my bruised ego started to heal and I landed a job, this time as an *"assistant* bookkeeper." It was, no doubt, a step backward. But the lessons learned under the tutelage of an experienced bookkeeper would lead to the proverbial "two steps forward." When I continued to be unhappy it dawned on me that I really didn't like bookkeeping after all.

I sought out and signed up for an aptitude testing program at NYU. There had to be a better way to make a living. After completing a series of tests that would certainly set me on the right track I anxiously awaited the results.

"It seems you have aptitudes for Engineering and Accounting," the counselor began. "Both, however, are highly sought after fields filled almost exclusively by men – with college degrees; I doubt you could get into or complete a difficult engineering program at this point. So let's see – you also showed some propensity for science. Lots of women are doing well as lab technicians or, if you are interested in travel, an airline stewardess may be a good idea. Those are two realistic alternatives I would advise. Good Luck to you."

Thanks a lot, I thought. The "Women's Liberation Movement" of the sixties wouldn't start for another few years. I continued work as a bookkeeper and after a one-year hiatus, half-heartedly returned to Baruch to pursue an Accounting degree. The Bachelor of Business Administration degree required 128 credits, half of which were in Business subjects. The other half consisted of English, Economics, Sociology other liberal arts subjects and a few electives. Survey courses in advertising and marketing caught my interest. I took both as electives and soon changed my major to Marketing.

There came a time late in 1959 when I found myself on unemployment for the second time. Like other institutions unemployment was different back then; the examiners, like "Jewish mothers" poured on the guilt. They looked at you like you were stealing food from the mouths of babies. You had to physically report every week – no calling it in. They looked you up and down to make sure you were dressed appropriately –business clothes, ready and able to work. Then they requested the list of potential employers you contacted and or were interviewed by for employment in the last week.

Finally, after a specified period, you had to visit the employment department. It worked the same way as a private employment agency except that no one ever found a job through it. It was considered another useless bureaucratic ritual that had to be endured as part of the punishment of being unemployed. So I certainly had no expectations. An examiner looked over my paperwork and asked:

"Susan, what kind of job are you looking for?"

I responded honestly, knowing there would be no such job in her files,

"What I would really like is a job as a bookkeeper in an advertising agency."

"Hmm," she replied "I think I saw something like that." She quickly thumbed through a stack of 3 x 5 index cards and there it was. A small business-to-business ad agency was looking for a full charge bookkeeper. It was a miracle. She called on the spot and sent me for an immediate interview.

So began my five years with Byrde, Richard and Pound. Their long-time full-charge bookkeeper was retiring. I was back in charge. Albeit I had to do more time as a bookkeeper, now under the thumb of Dan Filat.

He was a little man, literally and figuratively. In his mid-fifties, one day a month, he nervously ran into the office with his grey suit with its short pants and tiny jacket, a white shirt, and the lunch his mother packed for him. He would then proceed to drive me stark raving out of my mind.

"This column is off a penny, this is charged to the wrong account, you have to be more careful," he chided each and every month.

The days before he came were nerve-racking as I tried desperately to make sure everything was correct; that the totals of every column in every journal were correct and added up across the bottom of each page.

Thanks to Dan Filat I was committed to giving up bookkeeping. One spontaneous decision to take Advertising 101 had set me on a career course that I would enjoy for almost thirty years.

Chapter 49
Career Proceeds as Advertised

At Byrde, Richard and Pound for the first time I felt like I belonged. Although I was still buried in books, I was in an environment where copywriters, artists and idea people worked together to produce creative, persuasive communications. I was in my element.

Notwithstanding its compact size, this was a full service ad agency. As such, at any given time, we had three or four account executives, an art department with two full time artists, a production person, a media buyer and a one-girl receptionist-secretary-office manager. Leo Bernstein —"LB" was the "Pound" in the name and only remaining partner of what had been a larger organization. He was the boss and father figure. Bright, nurturing, in his mid-sixties, about 5'5" tall, white hair and blue eyes that, magnified by thick glasses, smiled good naturedly as he walked around the office.

He was also the primary Account Executive —the person who is responsible for everything about an account — often the person who sells the account on the agency. He managed a few long-term clients such as KitchenAid Dishwashers, Speed Queen Clothes Washers, and other now defunct companies. Another AE had several major book publishers among his accounts. For a short time an icon in the industry shared the office space. Roy Durstin of Batton, Barton, Durstine and Osborne, then in his eighties found a home here where he could still feel productive. He brought with him a few small accounts.

He was the first person I placed in my special imaginary "book" of people who I admired. He earned this place of honor based on his unaffected personality; by treating me, a nineteen year-old, as an equal — never talking down, always grateful for any little thing done on his behalf and treating everyone with the utmost respect. Unfortunately few people made my book and it eventually went by the wayside.

The congenial atmosphere lent itself to learning a little about a lot of aspects. I watched the artists quickly and skillfully sketch out a visual layout from a quick read of a proposed piece of copy and a few words with the account executive about the objective of an ad or literature piece; from time to time I proofread or typed copy and discussed it with the writers, I spent time with the media buyer and production manager – opportunities available only because of the size and nature of the business.

The practical experience dovetailed nicely with continuing classes as night, making me want more than ever to have a career in some aspect of advertising. I would do anything to get away from the month-after-month repetitiveness, nervous anticipation and dealing with Mr. Filat's picayune audit. After a year and a half I decided to leave and pursue something – anything – other than bookkeeping.

I still didn't have a clear direction or a college degree so my opportunities were limited. For some reason, and I still don't understand why, I set my sights on becoming a representative in an employment agency. I reasoned I would be in a position to deal with and help people.

I gave my notice. Mr. Bernstein asked what I had in mind. Amused by my plan he said "that's not for you; those places are "flesh pots. You have no idea what goes on with them."

His efforts to dissuade me failed and we parted ways. I put together a resume and made a valiant but futile effort to find a job in an agency. At the same time the young lady who took over my job wasn't working out. Mr. B. called me one day. We had an honest conversation and decided I would come back and, now more aware of my feelings, he would keep me in mind for something more palatable at the agency.

I returned the following week – back to the grind and Mr. Filat, my Nemesis. It wasn't long, however, before the media buyer decided to move to a larger agency and Mr. B. was good for his word. He gave me the position of Media Buyer. For a month or so I did two jobs, buying space and occasional radio spots for our clients and breaking in a new bookkeeper to take my place. The long days at work and evenings at school conspired to knock my resistance down and make way for a bad case of pneumonia to take hold.

Once things settled down I was in heaven. As a media buyer I had contact with media salespeople and clients. It meant long lunches, usually with a cocktail which was at first repugnant but soon made the meetings more relaxing. On the client side, it meant meeting with and discussing media objectives, options and optimal placements. These interactions resulted in new friendships.

Among them was a very special thirty year relationship with Laura, a young woman who worked in an office down the hall. She became a cherished lifelong friend and mentor. Laura and I started our days on the Lexington Avenue line; I boarded on 177th Street in the Bronx; she on 86th Street in Manhattan. We usually arrived at 28th Street at the same time, stopped for well buttered bialys and coffee from a vendor inside the subway station, and preceded to our respective offices on the fourth floor in the building across the street, 381 Park Avenue South.

Seven years my senior, Laura was like a big sister who accepted me as a friend and was a wise adviser at the same time. A connoisseur of cosmopolitan living, she introduced me to gourmet restaurants, eclectic foods, "Poully Fuisse" and "St.-Emilion," two of my favorite wines to this day.

We enjoyed each other's company, laughed until we cried. Through job changes, moves and marriages, our friendship grew and embraced friends, future husbands and families. We were each others' confidantes, co-conspirators and counselors for thirty years.

One evening, on the train going home after I had been attending college on and off, for about five years and accumulated a paltry forty, or so credits toward 128 I needed to graduate, Laura happened to ask, her voice pitched high to overcome the loud rattle of the train:

"So, how's it going at school these days?"

"I don't know. I'm thinking of forgetting about it; I'll just never finish."

"Why would you quit now" she questioned further, unable to mask her shock.

In some way Laura was going to college vicariously through me; she was very bright and regretted not having continued her education.

"Even if I go every semester from now on and take nine credits at a time, I'll be thirty by the time I graduate," I whined.

Then, from Laura's lips came an epiphany that changed my life.

"Aren't you going to be thirty whether you graduate or not?" she asked.

From then on I registered every semester for 9-12 credits, often attending four nights a week. Finally in 1969, a little more than ten years from when I started and two months after my thirtieth birthday, I received a Bachelor of Business Administration degree in Marketing from Bernard Baruch College.

Laura and I remained friends until I lost her to the pall of "Pall Mall" cigarettes which she refused to give up even as their dangers became more well-known. She passed away at the untimely age of fifty-seven. She is still very much alive for me every day, not only because of our relationship, but also because what she said to me on that trip home altered the course of my life from that day forward.

Part V
1960s – Turning Points

Chapter 50
Decade of Change—Defining Moments

The sixties were best known for protests, revolution and yes, some major achievements. Feminists burned their bras, Vietnam War protestors burned draft cards and the civil rights movement introduced sit-ins and race riots. John F. Kennedy was the youngest person and first catholic to be elected President. His life was taken in the first of three high profile assassinations including those of Martin Luther King and Robert Kennedy. In 1969 Neil Armstrong, one of our original astronauts landed on the moon and summed up the milestone with his oft repeated quote:

"That's one small step for man, one giant leap for mankind."

It's fair to say that the country and the world experienced major changes from 1960 to 1969. Albeit on a much smaller scale so did our family.

I turned twenty-one, the age of majority, in March 1960. I was already on my fourth job. At our company Christmas party in 1959 just months before my birthday and days before the new decade, coworkers had a good laugh when they refused to allow me an alcoholic beverage because I had not yet reached the legal drinking age in New York.

Wouldn't you know it, the age of majority was changed to eighteen in the fall of 1960 largely because eighteen year-old boys were being drafted into the service; legislators under pressure from the citizenry, reasoned that if a boy could fight and get killed he should be able to get a drink. The drinking age in New York has bounced back and forth over the years and is currently twenty one again.

The uncertainty of the draft hung over young men. They had to register as soon as they turned eighteen at which time they were assigned a number. The lower the number the sooner they could expect to be drafted making it difficult to move ahead with their lives. Two male friends, Marty and Tiny were classified 4F, a medical classification. Arnie, however, was classified "1A" and assigned a relatively low number.

After graduation from Roosevelt, he enrolled at City College to study accounting. It was hard to commit to school while anticipating a notice from Uncle Sam any day. After his second year he pushed up his draft and was inducted into the Army in the fall of 1959 and shipped off to Jackson South Carolina for basic training. He and Roz, who had a clerical job that she hated, were going steady by then. Within six months, in May 1960, he at age twenty and she having just turned twenty-one tied the knot.

By March 1961 Mark was born. Starting a family on a PFC salary was very difficult. Based on his accounting studies he was assigned to the finance department, a position that helped him get a job on Wall Street upon his discharge at the end of 1962. Soon after, they moved to a project in Staten Island.

Other friends married too. Brenda wed her sailor boyfriend who was seven years older as soon as she graduated from Roosevelt in June 1957. Her daughter Arlene came along in August of '58. At the time if a girl wasn't married by the time she was twenty-two, family and friends desperately arranged blind dates and pulled out all the stops to make sure she would not remain an old maid.

Marriage was not a high priority for me. I was focused on building a better future. Besides I had witnessed bad marriages between Mom and Dad and others. Mama bad-mouthed the institution. She didn't like to go to weddings:

"They don't know each other or how it will turn out and they make a big party. No. I'll be happy to go to their tenth anniversary party."

That kind of talk was not very encouraging. It also didn't hurt that the guys weren't knocking down doors to get to me. I still had a few single friends and made new ones through work and school and we enjoyed being unattached in New York: Broadway, dining in some of the best restaurants and motor trips were much more attractive than changing diapers, listening to screaming babies and dealing with husbands at that stage of life.

During the summer from time-to-time we enjoyed weekend "cruises to nowhere," our first taste of cruising. They left the dock on the West side on Friday night after work, sailed three miles out to sea – into international waters where inexpensive liquor flowed freely and gambling was legal.

My first one was on a Greek Ship where the crew members all looked like Greek Gods with dark complexions, curly black hair and brown eyes and well developed six packs. "Ouzo," a licorice flavored liqueur, was 35 cents a shot. Bands played and entertainers took to the stage — all the stuff of a cruise except without ports of call. We savored great epicurean delights, dancing and well stocked, artistically arranged midnight buffets. On Monday morning the ship docked in the city and we were off to work to begin a new week.

In August of 1960 Ann, Sybil and I joined Marty, a neighborhood guy who originally hung out with Shirley before attaching himself to our group, on a trip to Florida. He had just purchased a new American Motors "Javelin" that we took turns driving. What was usually a two day trip from New York to Miami took us five days.

While we enjoyed the route, that ran as close to the east coast shore as possible, it was hot in mid-July. By 3:00 PM each day we stopped at a nice motel and quickly took to the cool swimming pool. Then it was off to the best restaurant we could find, usually followed by a nightcap if there was a cocktail lounge nearby.

We stayed overnight in Virginia Beach, North Carolina — then home to a naval base and crawling with handsome sailors. Next stop was Myrtle Beach, South Carolina where we got our first taste of southern hospitality and succulent porterhouse steak. Then it was on to Jacksonville, Florida where we visited the Fiskeys who had recently relocated there. From there we spent a day and night in West Palm Beach, before reaching our destination in Miami Beach.

There wasn't a lot for us to do there. We spent our days at the pool or beach where I got burnt to a crisp. One day a young fellow came to the pool to sell us on water skiing lessons. Being a very weak swimmer I was reluctant to try it.

"Oh," he said, "you'll do fine. The lessons are given in very shallow water and the instructor is at your side the whole time."

The minute I agreed, he turned to everyone in the pool and urged them to try a lesson.

"It's very safe, even she signed up," he pointed at me.

On the appointed day, I slathered suntan lotion all over my body — a fair skinned redhead I burned just thinking about sun. The first thing that happened was they lined us all up and announced:

"If anyone has suntan lotion on, there is Ajax on the back table — use it to take every drop of lotion off." The speaker explained that the instructor would be holding onto our thighs and "the suntan lotion will make you slippery and we could lose you if his hand slips."

About a dozen people lined up, were given skis and shown how to put them on. The first few were taken out by an instructor and did fairly well – one or two ended up in the boat. When my turn came I went under almost immediately and the handsome young instructor couldn't wait to put me in the boat. After the first round, those of us in the boat were taken off and placed in the bleachers to watch as the lessons continued.

Before long I observed *my* instructor with a female student who was striking: with long blonde hair, 5'6" tall and what appeared to be better than perfect "36, 24", 36." My lower measurements weren't too different. The top one, however, was by about four inches and somehow the package was more attractive to the male of the species. Mr. Instructor, a big smile now plastered on his face, rescued her time and again as she too went down. An older man sitting next to me who had witnessed the entire lesson felt bad for me.

"He didn't give you a chance, I'd be happy to show you the right way to water ski."

I looked at my scraped shins and replied,

"no thank you, I think I've had enough of water skis for a lifetime."

The hurt that resulted from my athletic failure was assuaged in the evening. It was our practice to have a nice dinner and stop for a drink in the hotel lounge afterward. We went to some first-rate restaurants and some lesser ones. Wolfie's delicatessen was one of the latter. I had franks and beans there one day. Then we had a drink or two as we listened to a string of old people jokes in the lounge. Something did not agree with me as evidenced by the number of times I tasted the beans while I spent the rest of the evening heaving my guts up.

Our hopes of running into some handsome guys were dashed. There weren't many young single men around and we were probably the youngest people in the hotel.

Ten days after we set out from home by car, we girls boarded a plane for the first time, leaving Marty behind to drive his car back. We had spent all of our money. When the stewardess – as attendants were called before males entered the field and political correctness eliminated titles that alluded to gender – asked us if we wanted something to drink we declined; we didn't know if there was a charge for a cup of coffee and didn't want to be embarrassed.

Shirley and Gerry waited for us when we disembarked. We were so happy to see them. We weren't sure how we were going to get home without a dime to our collective names? Florida turned out to be the first of many car trips up and down the East and West coasts.

When we weren't on the road, we went to dances, singles bars and the occasional singles resort – we wanted to have a good time with the hope of meeting Mr. Right. On one weekend at a dude ranch it actually worked for my friend Lorraine who met her husband. Sydelle, too, met Aaron at a Lakeville, NJ singles bar and Marty met Roz many years later at a dance. Often these venues were humiliating. There was lots of tension; people were not themselves; for the most part, they were on the defensive which frequently led to hurtful comments. Still there were few options for meeting people of the opposite gender. Other common venues were the neighborhood, school or work – the internet was decades into the future.

On the home front things continued to move along relatively quietly. Dad and I continued to work while Mom kept the home fires burning – much easier now since we had converted to gas heat and hot water. She continued to entertain drop-ins although their numbers were beginning to decline – some passed away, others stopped coming because of age-related ailments, still others began to move to other neighborhoods because of a series of changes that were eroding ours.

Our family changed as well, with the addition of baby Julia born October 14, 1960 as a member of the Beck/Sherman clan. A year later, Ross made his way into the world in Pennsylvania. By mid-decade, on New Year's Eve 1965, Benny, Doris, Ned, Brad and Ross hailed the arrival of Lynn into the family, bringing the total number of grandchildren for Mom and Dad to six.

Chapter 51
Beginning of the End

Our East Tremont neighborhood — a longtime community where hard working people knew each other, kept up their homes and gardens, and apartment dwellers with deep roots in the area lived quietly in their affordable apartments — began to change in the early 1960s.

In our case fewer and fewer of the eccentric characters that had become part of the family wandered in and out of the house. Store keepers began to move. Mom was forced to shop in the supermarkets that she so detested.

"I never saw anything like it. They don't look at you:" she complained, "they pick up each package, put the price into the cash register and push the product along. Then they throw everything in a bag, take the money and start over without ever looking at the customer."

Mama yearned for the bygone camaraderie of the proprietors and other customers— the social banter, the personal touch. When she was forced to purchase pre-packaged products, she would have given anything to be able to buy fresh sliced American cheese, tub butter, and a fresh rye bread. She hungered for the time not long before when she was able to custom pick the cut of beef for fresh ground meat; had a choice of steaks and chops to pick from. When her butcher moved to the West Bronx, I drove her there every few weeks and she stocked up as much as she could.

The transformation was slow but steady. Construction of the Cross Bronx Expressway was accelerated. Protests by neighborhood activists and political infighting had been taking place for years. But the building of sections of the highway was already underway in various locations.

The seven mile highway built to connect the eastern part of the state with points west gutted the heart of the Bronx. A few blocks away from our home, tenants were forced to vacate apartment buildings; the buildings were razed and noise, fumes and dust filled the air to make way for what turned out to be and still is one of the worst thoroughfares in the country. Jon Bruner, in a post on www.forbes.com in 2009 about the country's worst intersections and how they affect lifestyle, wrote more than forty years later:

"The Cross Bronx Expressway, that fume-choked expanse of concrete and steel that slices through New York City's mainland borough, occupies a uniquely tragic place in the history of urban planning.'

'It displaced more than 60,000 middle-class residents during its construction between 1948 and 1963, and it cost $250 million--more than any highway project before it. The apartment buildings that line its growling trench have been home to generations of asthmatic children who struggle to breathe in the acrid clouds of exhaust that fill the air. Its presence has so thoroughly eviscerated its surroundings that many blocks adjacent to it are occupied entirely by families living below the poverty level.'

'The so-called "Cross Bronx" can add another ignominious distinction to its long list: Exit 4B is home to America's worst intersection, according to traffic-tracking firm Inrix. In fact, three of America's four worst bottlenecks are interchanges on its seven-mile length."

Of the 60,000 residents that were displaced by this debacle, many moved to other locations in the Bronx; others relocated to adjoining boroughs, and still others took refuge in nearby New Jersey, the suburbs in Westchester and Long Island as well as locations far away from their cherished Bronx neighborhoods.

Korean War veterans joined their World War II brothers and their young families in the suburbs which were being quickly built. In 1962, Shirley and Gerry were among them; they found a small ranch style house in a new development in Central Islip.

Neighbors migrated to the west Bronx, New Jersey or Queens. Mom sorely missed Mrs. Eifler, who gave into her growing fear as her co-tenants fled, was one of the last to move out of her top floor apartment to higher ground in the West Bronx. It was the beginning of the end. Mom and Dad didn't want to give up the house; nobody bothered us personally.

We stayed.

Groups of low-income people, most African American and Puerto Rican, filled the vacancies in the apartment buildings. Properties began to fall into disrepair. Landlords, bound by rent control laws, couldn't afford or refused to make repairs because the new tenants misused the property. Drug use and crime exploded throughout the area.

We stayed.

We worried about Dad coming home late at night after working fourteen hours. Mom and I often went to the station on West Farms Road to look for him. We breathed a sigh of relief when we saw him safely making his way up the hill.

Beck's farm of the forties slowly ceased to be a meeting place for friends, neighbors and lonely sojourners who gradually stopped coming by. Mom spent more time reading and tending her garden while her social network narrowed. The produce man, the grocer and the baker were supplanted by supermarkets, our once busy street became less hospitable and a sense of anxiety hung over the community.

Still, we stayed.

Chapter 52
Dad Loses Heart

Early in 1964, Dad's slow deliberate steps as he walked up the hill from the station, along with shortness of breath led him to a visit with Dr. Mishuris, the family doctor. He listened to Dad's heart, took and EKG and asked:

"So tell me, Mr. Beck, have you had any chest pain lately?"

"I have had some difficulty breathing and I occasionally feel some tightness in my chest, but that's about it," Dad responded.

The EKG and examination indicated that he probably suffered a minor heart attack sometime earlier; his heart showed scar tissue indicating that there had been an occlusion of an artery that had caused damage and reduced efficiency. The heart was enlarged as a result of having to work harder.

There was no way to fix it. The only course of action was to try to prevent further attacks and damage.

"Harry, you have to slow down – no overexertion; you must cut back on fat and eliminate all salt from your diet," the doctor admonished.

Fat chance. Mom had always kept our fat intake to a minimum so that wasn't difficult. Salt was another story – she used it sparingly but even that was too much. Artificial salt, available in drug stores, had a chemical taste. We tried every brand. No way would Dad eat anything with even a hint of it.

"It's better to die than have to eat that stuff" he said as he pushed his food away.

As for exertion, Dad was not about to slack off; as always his *business was on the verge of taking off.*

For the next few months he went on as usual – angina and shortness of breath continued but he pushed through it.

His symptoms gradually worsened; each week Dr. Mishuris heard the sounds of continuing deterioration and degradation. EKG's confirmed more damage and he eventually recommended a cardiologist.

"A good cardiologist is like a great virtuoso who can hear the difference between a Stradivarius and an ordinary violin. I think it's time to see what he has to say."

The Cardiologist confirmed that Dad's heart was indeed very weak. Before long his condition progressed to Congestive Heart Failure where the heart muscle weakens to the point where it can't pump hard enough to push blood through the body. At that point a couple of things happen. First, not enough oxygen is delivered to the body, so muscles that don't get enough oxygen tire more quickly making it harder to walk or climb stairs. Every organ in the body needs an adequate oxygen supply and blood circulation and when the heart fails to meet those needs, the body gradually shuts down. Fluid starts backing up because the heart can't keep it moving. The fluid backs up into the lungs, making it increasingly hard to breath, and edema in the peripheral tissues causes feet, ankles, and legs to swell.

Not being able to breathe was the hardest symptom for dad to bear. It was at its worst in bed at night; his lungs filled when he lied on his back. He would jump out of bed, open the window and gasp for air. Mom and I panicked and frequently called the doctor in the middle of the night. He came regardless of the time and gave Dad a shot that miraculously eased the situation in minutes.

Still for many months Dad was in and out of the hospital – he received oxygen and medications for a few days and then come home. On some of those occasions he was transported by private ambulance – sirens blasting.

The time came when Dr. Mishuris came to the house every day to check on him. At his recommendation I bought a bottle of Cognac every payday at a liquor store conveniently located steps from the train station.

"A few shots are good for the heart," the doctor told us – now that was a medicine Dad could take.

By this time he was no longer able to make it to the shop so one Saturday morning, with directions from him, my good friend Sybil and I drove down, and packed up Dad's final dream. We boxed inventory and equipment for distribution to nearby shopkeepers and the sanitation department and brought few cartons home. We made several elevator trips to complete the job.

At one point Sybil opened the passenger car door and placed her handbag on the front seat; she then joined me to continue loading the trunk. Within minutes her bag was gone; Sybil had a tendency to carry her life in her bag so it was a big loss. She refused my offer to at least replace the some $300.00 in cash. That day we suffered a tangible loss but also learned, unfortunately, that given the slightest opportunity evil seems to be on the ready to rip you off.

On the flip side, during this tough time, the value of good friends was reinforced. Costs of daily doctor's visits, though very low by current standards, mounted up along with other related expenses. After paying Doctor Mishuris forty-to-fifty dollars per week for several months, four well-meaning friends, Ann, Sybil, Irene and Elaine became concerned about the drain on my finances; behind my back they went to see the doctor and offered to pay him to relieve me of this burden. He accepted their offer and they swore him to secrecy. He continued his daily visits and I left him weekly checks.

In the course of routine conversation they began to ask me—

"are you still paying Doctor Mishuris every week?"

"Sure," I responded, "why wouldn't I?" Finally, one of them confessed.

I couldn't believe my ears and immediately went to his office to confront him:

"Are you taking money from my friends?" He casually responded "yes."

"First of all, where do you come off doing that? And, secondly why are you still taking payments from me?"

His response was more astonishing than the act.

"I was crediting it to your account for when you run out."

I saw red. The next morning I called the American Medical Association (AMA) to report him and they dissuaded me from pursuing a complaint since I would have a hard time making a case. But that was the end of Dr. M. as Dad's doctor.

It was a decision I continue to question to this very day. As much as he may have been unprofessional, his daily visits seemed to be therapeutically beneficial. His presence provided some degree of hope for Dad.

I switched to a younger doctor with whom Dad never bonded. After coming in from Westchester once or twice to give Dad the shot that drained his lungs as he continued to gasp for air in the middle of many nights, the new doctor prescribed long acting pills that didn't act as quickly. I'll never know if my decision hastened Dad's demise but it wouldn't be long before his condition, both physically and spiritually, drastically declined.

I would find him sitting on the stoop, teary eyed.

"What is it?" I'd ask.

"Oh nothing, I'm just thinking about my life. I could have done many things differently. I let you all down" There was no consoling him.

Shirley and the family visited often on weekends and he got a charge out the childish antics of Neil and Julie, six and four respectively. Benny and Doris came up for a visit. Benny took the boys to the park and hoisted them onto the big rock at the entrance for the mandatory photo.

Dad could no longer join them at the zoo but he cherished the little time he had with his grandchildren – their short visits invigorated his failing heart.

Chapter 53
The Horror of Halloween 1964

As was his custom during the last nine months, Dad woke up on the morning of October 31, 1964, had his oat meal and coffee and walked to the candy store to pick up the "New York Times." He returned home, spread the paper on the dining room table and began to read it while Mom sat opposite him on the recliner engrossed in the "Home News."

In minutes, she heard a thump and looked up to see Dad sliding from the chair onto the floor. I was still asleep upstairs when I heard her scream. I jumped out of bed and ran downstairs to find Mom standing over Dad who was now lying on the floor, his head propped against the chair leg. I bent down, placed his head on my arm, shook him, and pleaded with him to talk to us. But it was too late. He was gone.

Mom and I held each other for several minutes.

"It's the two of us now," I whispered trying to calm her.

Then I called the police and Ann who still lived only a few blocks away.

Ann and her brother Norman, also a great friend, arrived within moments to help comfort us. The police too arrived relatively quickly. Their presence alone was reassuring. They guided us through the process that accompanies such an incident. A short time later, Dad's remains were removed to the funeral home.

Shirley, Gerry and the kids arrived as well and together we took care of arrangements.

All the time children were ringing the bell. I rarely write poetry although I envy the ability of poets to capture nature, romance beauty and often the profundity of life with a remarkable economy of words. Clearly, it is not my forte. In certain circumstances, however, I find myself trying to use poetry to illustrate something I find humorous, ironic or too perplexing to express in prose. Occasionally it allows me to better articulate deep emotions. If there was ever a time in my life that I needed to exploit this writing form this was it. The events of that day elicited the following poem:

Halloween 1964

Goblins, ghosts, witches and pirates roamed the street
Little voices declared: "trick or treat!"
Bells chimed, small knuckles knocked, beckoned us to the door
They had always been greeted with a smile and a sweet before.

But this year was different in a way they could not dream
For that very morning I woke to Mom's blood curdling scream
I ran to see a once familiar face now more frightening than any mask
On the floor, lay my Dad – his eyes wide open, shocked, aghast.
I quickly knelt, his head in my arm— asked for a word, a sign
Instead I heard a rattle as his body lie supine
At that moment I knew Dad drew his last breath
For he had told me of the final resonance of his own father's death
Strong, vibrant, funny Dad a lifeless puppet – flaccid, strangely still
Like lightening whisked away – perhaps to a so-called hereafter
Forever stripped of his earthly spirit – his laughter

Ever since – each Halloween I don my mask
Hide the memory of that Halloween long past
Greet my young guests with a smile and a treat.
Bury my ghostly reflection until next Halloween

Chapter 54
Road Bump Jolts Career

A tsunami swept our entire staff back out into the job pool. Almost all of the fourteen loyal employees, who had worked for the company from five to twenty years, left within six months.

The disaster that struck our small congenial ad agency was a new partner. My problems with him started before the partnership even became official. One Saturday morning at about 8:30AM the phone rang. Mama woke me:

"Your boss is on the phone" she said with a quizzical expression.

My boss? He never called me at home before, I thought in the fog of sleep. I picked up the receiver. It wasn't my boss; it was Mr. Grrrr, my soon-to-be boss He announced himself.

"Hi Susan, this is Eliot. I want to talk to you about some changes we will be making and I'd be interested in your input. I would like you to write up the current procedures: how work flows, forms, approvals and anything else you can think of and bring the information in on Monday. We will be meeting at 9:00AM sharp."

I was dumfounded – number one, I was not the office manager (we didn't have one), two he wasn't even part of the organization yet and three why couldn't this wait. I don't remember how or if I replied but he was already on my *Sh_ _ list*, defined by the American Heritage dictionary as a "list of persons who are strongly disapproved of."

His position on said list was confirmed when, on another occasion some time later, he ordered me to stay late – as late as necessary to complete a project by the next morning.

"I'm sorry, I explained, "that could take all night and it's uncalled for. I can finish it tomorrow."

"I said it must be done tonight – if you get tired you can nap on the cot in the break room," he shot back.

He had moved a cot in for just such situations; to date it had only been used by him and his stalwart assistant who had joined us as part the package. I was livid. Looking right into his eyes I put my fingers under the bottom edge of the relatively new "IBM Selectric" typewriter in front of me and flipped it onto the floor where it landed at his feet.

"I don't sleep on the job," I said and walked away.

I thought that was it. I didn't care; I had enough and was sure he would want me out of there ASAP. Seconds later, he murmured:

"I'm sorry if I upset you, but this is an important client and I don't want to take a chance on missing a deadline."

"I have been doing this for quite some time and have never missed a deadline — and I never had to sleep in the office to finish a project."

"OK, can we just put this behind us?" he asked. I shot back:

"I'm afraid not. I think this is a good time for me to give you my two weeks notice."

"I can't accept your notice."

"Fine, I'll just leave right now." We continued back and forth and in the end negotiated four weeks notice.

The weeks passed slowly. As the only one handling media, I alerted Kathy, Mr. Grrrr's assistant about current client schedules, outstanding orders for which placements had to be verified and upcoming orders to be processed soon after my departure.

As for Mr. Grrrr himself, I avoided him like the plague, responding only to his occasional greeting. How one as bright, efficient and congenial as Kathy could work with him never ceased to baffle me.

Equally bewildering, after acting impulsively as I had, was what I would do next. Naturally, I began telling salesmen, vendors and clients that I would be leaving the agency. One of the clients with whom I had established a good working relationship suggested I join her company. It was a family business that manufactured photo-sensitive films used in screen printing, lithography and electronic photo circuit production. The firm maintained a main office and two factories in Brownsville, Brooklyn.

My first reaction was no way would I work in Brooklyn, no less the section in which the office was located. A well known New York journalist Jimmy Breslin wrote a few years later, that Brownsville reminded him of Berlin after World War II; "block after block of burned-out shells of houses, streets littered with decaying automobile hulks. The stores are empty and the streets are lined with deserted apartment houses or buildings that have empty apartments on every floor."

Marion, my future employer, took care of my dilemma before I voiced it.

"I rarely go to the factories" she explained; Bernie, my brother, handles that part of the business. I do all the rest and I really could use some help with the marketing and advertising. I'm thinking you could work here in my apartment."

Her co-op was on the 21st floor of a luxury building on East End Avenue and 89th Street – across the street from the Mayor's official residence – Gracie Mansion. We set up a quick meeting and sealed the deal.

It turned out to be quite an experience. Marion was a bubbly, outgoing, charismatic woman ten years my senior. We placed a 4' x 8' half-inch furniture grade plywood panel atop two-three drawer file cabinets back-to-back at either end, and voila we had a work station for two. We sat across from each other, face-to-face, for the next three years before moving to new quarters nearby.

For me the turmoil created by Mr. Grrrr meant a giant leap from my job at an ad agency to the client side. My new job was to work with Marion to develop a plan for all marketing communications including sales brochures, flyers, trade publication advertising and trade show materials. She was a natural salesperson; I brought to the table, everything I was studying at school and what I had picked up from my agency experience with other clients. Together we developed plans and budgets and oversaw all marketing communications. I had come a long way; from recording numbers to being responsible for a $200,000 budget.

I worked with a growing number of outside vendors including my old ad agency, photographers, printers and producers of trade show exhibits. I flew around the country setting up and working our booths with salesmen and managers.

My time with Marion wasn't all work and no play. She and I shared funny stories and jokes, often with the savoir faire of truck drivers; she made great lunches too – in the midst of what was the German section of the city – she served big juicy knockwurst, the best liverwurst in town and tasty crab soufflés, as well as excellent iced coffee with honey and the occasional vodka gimlet after a hard day's work.

There was no drinking,, however, on the days I drove Marion to Aqueduct Raceway or the Tamoshanter Golf Club in Glen Cove, Long Island in her 1965 powder blue Cadillac. I loved driving in general but this car transformed me. No only did I feel like a millionaire behind the wheel, I was also powerful and became a road bully.

After I dropped her off I went back to work alone, or with Mildred, the housekeeper who was there several times a week.

An avid golfer, Marion had putters and practice putting paraphernalia in the living room so from time-to-time I took a break and tried my hand at getting a hole in one.

I spent a lot of time alone at the apartment as Marion travelled for business and vacations. It could get quite lonely especially because when she was home we had a good time together.

After five years this dream job would also come to a crashing end. Still it was great while it lasted. As it turned out I had Mr.Grrrr to thank for it. He forced me into a pivotal position that took me from ad agency side of advertising to the client side where I was truly involved with every one of the myriad aspects of marketing a product.

I think of Marion often. She was, without a doubt, one of the best bosses I ever had. Nor will I ever forget that unique work experience or its impact on my bumpy career path through a diverse, interesting and gratifying ride.

Chapter 55
Generation—III All Americans

The third generation that resulted from the union Zalman and Suzan Bak in 1882 was complete in the late sixties. Ben and Doris's, Lynn and their three boys, ages three-to-seven lived in rural York County, Pennsylvania. We visited them sporadically. No matter where they lived, both Ben and Doris were into gardening and in summer they always had a nice crop of corn and beds of lovely flowers.

Ben worked in a variety of jobs before he finally settled into selling Kirby Vacuum Cleaners. Like Dad and the farm, this seemed an unlikely occupation for Ben but he seemed to really get into it. He liked the interaction with consumers and with his easy personality he made a living at it.

Ned and Brad were both the serious, quiet types – at least when we were visiting.

From the time Ross was able to talk, when asked what he wanted to be, he responded without hesitation:

"I want to be an army man." So when he joined the Marines after graduating from high school it came as no surprise. Brad, too, served in the Air Force – at this writing so too have two of his five children.

And Lynn was a beautiful little girl. I thought as a child she looked a lot like her Dad; she was certainly the apple of his eye.

Shirley, Gerry, Neil and Julie had settled into their home on Long Island. Gerry worked as a job shopper which meant he was away for long periods to work on contracts as a draftsman/engineer. He earned a good living when he worked but there were often long stretches between jobs so cash ebbed and flowed.

Their home was about fifty miles from ours so we visited each other quite frequently. We celebrated birthdays and holidays together along with Gerry's parents. Gerry's father, Gerry and Julie all shared an October 14th birthday so there was always a big party to celebrate all three of them.

The Shermans enjoyed their suburban home and community. Most of the families were close in age and the kids had lots of friends as did Shirley.

Not long after Neil started school, however, some of the other kids began to bully him. There were few Jews in the area and for some reason religion did not come up as a problem until he began attending school. Then kids taunted him using religious slurs.

Shirley and Gerry were loving, attentive parents; some might have considered them overprotective in many ways. Their response was to take him out of the negative environment – one might say he almost took after his Aunt Susie (AKA Aunt Louie so named because he couldn't say Susie.) Like me he became an early dropout. I think, however, he made it to second grade before dropping out.

His parents proceeded to take him out of public school and enroll him in the Hebrew Academy of Long Island, a private parochial school. Shirley worked in the office to cover the cost of tuition for both Neil and Julie who was starting kindergarten.

Rabbi Maza who ran the school was from a family of rabbis; one of whom later became rather well known as a comedian under the name of Jackie Mason. As it happened, Neil's Bar Mitzvah in 1971 came out during one of Gerry's job-seeking periods making a traditional celebration impractical. Instead the festivities took place in a local synagogue under the direction of another of Rabbi Maza's brothers. The entire school attended; Neil eloquently conducted the Bar Mitzvah service, and then the students, family and friends feasted on bagels and lox – a good time was had by all.

The kids seemed to enjoy their new school, Shirley, too, liked working at the Hebrew Academy.

We heard from Ben and Doris that their kids were doing well at school too. They were active in sports and the school band. They obviously acquired musical talent from Doris's side of the family.

The Beck/Sherman/Jones branches of the family, including the third generation for Zalman and Suzan Bak, were fully assimilated into the American Mosaic.

Chapter 56
Two Women Alone in an Urban Wasteland

Mom and I continued to live in one of the city's many decaying neighborhoods. Ironically we had upgraded the house itself with the help of a $2,600.00 bank loan and Oscar our old superintendent from 178th Street who now lived down the block and did the work.

We renovated the kitchen, adding Oscar's hand made wood hanging cabinets, florescent lighting and new appliances. We redid the bathroom, replacing the toilet, sink and vintage claw foot tub where I had hidden cigarette butts years earlier — and installed our first shower. At my insistence, we also discarded many of the old fixtures and features including the cherub designs around the light fixtures throughout the house. In hindsight I think maybe I should have listened to Mama when she was resolute about their future value as antiques; especially when I see similar ones coming back into vogue. Finally we painted the interior and the back porch.

The restoration brought us back to the dollhouse charm of 25 years earlier when we moved in. Our refurbished home, however, was like a golden calla lily in the middle of a landfill. All around used syringes, whiskey bottles, beer cans and other trash littered the street. We tried to go on as if nothing had changed and in many ways we succeeded. Mom continued to tend her garden with its spring crocus, daffodils and tulips — red, pink and golden roses of summer — and fall's mums in an array of mauves, yellows, and rust colors.

I continued my grind of work by day and school by night. Each morning I went from what resembled war-torn Berlin to the promenades of the upper east side of Manhattan. On New Years Day 1966 the city had its first transit strike ever. It crippled all manner of activity for twelve days; there was no train or bus service. From day one on, a limousine pulled onto our block strewn with grime, broken down cars and debris. The driver pulled up in front of our house, picked me up and we were off to East End Avenue. At the end of the day I became Cinderella when the chariot dropped me back home.

Home now was just two women, abandoned even by the authorities. Occasionally we needed the fire department to turn off the hydrant directly opposite the house on the other side of the street. On hot summer evenings, teenagers, and sometimes adults, turned them on too cool off. They removed the tops and bottoms of metal coffee, soda and food cans and used them to direct the flow of ice cold water into the air while young children and whoever else was so inclined jumped in to cool off; unfortunately the water came through our poorly sealed windows and we slipped and slid on the stairs. When I called for help the firemen around the corner either did not respond or arrived a half-hour later with a fully staffed truck, sirens blasting, and wrenches in hand to defend themselves. It came to a point when I stopped calling, made my way through the cascading water and pleaded my case directly to the kids at the hydrant.

"I know you don't mean to cause any harm but the water is coming directly into our windows across the street; it's dangerous. Please give me the cans."

"Sorry," the rabble rousers said; they gave me the cans and moved on.

They were just kids like I had been some twenty years before. Back then after letting us have a half-hour of fun, a single fireman walked around the corner from the firehouse and turned off the water. He smiled and explained that the open hydrant decreased the water pressure that might be needed in case a fire broke out somewhere nearby. Often we turned it back on minutes after he left; he came back and turned it off again. Sometimes this went on for a few rounds.

The police, too, became unresponsive. There were evenings when a bunch of wise guy kids repeatedly rang the doorbell, ran a stick back and forth along the fence, or brawled in front of the house to get a rise out of Mama. On rare occasions I called the police to disburse them. If and when they arrived an hour or so after the call, the kids were long gone. The responding officers strongly advised us to move.

"What are you still doing here?" They asked incredulously. "You don't belong here anymore. Move far away from here."

They were right. Every time I came home late at night I felt a knot in my stomach. When I parked my car and had to make my way to the house, I heard imaginary footsteps behind me and was afraid to look back. On the four block walk from the subway after evening classes at City College in Manhattan I held a key between my fingers ready to poke out the eyes of a would be attacker. When I saw young men and women physically trade punches on the streets I held my breath and looked the other way, trying to make myself invisible lest they involve me somehow. Surprisingly, neither Mama nor I was ever directly threatened.

"Where will we go? Nobody is hurting us here," Mama would say when I urged her to consider moving.

Despite everything going on around us, Mama seemed to have what was probably a false sense of security as well as an almost irrational passionate attachment to the house both of which caused us to stay too long at the farm, albeit not Beck's farm of the forties and fifties.

Chapter 57
Bronx Tale Closing Moments

Despite her growing loneliness and increasing uneasiness associated with living in a gradually decaying environment, Mom continued to maintain the household and enjoy reasonably good health.

She was in her early sixties and had so far escaped major medical problems. Shirley and I always worried that her eating habits, sans teeth, would someday catch up with her digestive system.

Her first hospitalization, however, at sixty-four had nothing to do with that. It was for a "vaginal prolapse," a common female condition in which the uterus drops as a result of weakened muscles. It is usually, but not always, associated with aging as well as the number, timing and nature of past pregnancies.

After suffering discomfort for about a year, not to mention associated, sometimes humorous embarrassments, Mom opted for surgery to correct the situation from which she recovered quickly.

Three years later, however, she started to have frequent and severe abdominal pain, nausea and explosive vomiting. The family doctor suspected gallbladder disease which, in 1969, was difficult to diagnose; it wasn't until years later that new scanning techniques enabled positive diagnoses.

My friend Elaine recommended a highly regarded surgeon who specialized in gastroenterology and cancer. He confirmed the need for surgery to remove Mom's gallbladder. She underwent the surgery in New York Hospital in Manhattan and Dr. Booher was elated when he did not find any cancer despite his early strong suspicion.

"Everything is OK. I explored her entire gastric system and it is clean" he reported as he emerged after the operation.

Following the surgery, she was weak and uncomfortable for months; we didn't think too much of it because recovery from gallbladder surgery was known to be long, painful and difficult. Her debility continued and she never really regained her former strength.

It was then that she decided it would be a good idea to sell the house and move on. I believe she anticipated her own mortality and feared for my safety.

She didn't want to leave me with the burden of living there alone and having to handle a move by myself.

We put the house on the market and had a few bites. One that was particularly promising was from a young African American family who made an offer. We just couldn't get ourselves to go through with a deal advising them instead to wait and spend some time in the area before making a final decision. After that we gave the listing to a realtor.

For the next several months we looked at apartments.

"This is the whole apartment?" Mama asked, tears welling up in her eyes when we looked at what seemed like dozens of garden apartments in Queens where the entrance was typically into a small living room.

In another case to see if Mom might like the amenities, we looked at a co-op apartment which my friends Sydelle and Aaron had been living in for some time.

"Not bed" ("bad" with a Jewish accent) Mom said to spare their feelings. The phrase has become an inside joke between Aaron and me ever since.

The truth was that many of the apartments had as much living space as our house but no apartment would ever take the place of Mom's little doll house.

Our search also took us to Co-op City which was soon to be completed. We looked at models of two-bedroom apartments in the high rise buildings as well as the few townhouses they had also built. Everything was new, large and quite nice but neither of us cared for the idea of so many people living together in a closed community.

In the fall of 1969 we sold the house to a speculator for $12,000.00. The sales process was somewhat complicated because Dad, in one of his characteristic trusting acts, handled the closing by himself without benefit of an attorney. It turned out that in an estate sale, all possible beneficiaries had to sign away their rights to the property. The routine title search showed no affidavits to that effect.

I, who had obviously inherited some of his traits, hired a schoolmate's husband who had just passed the Bar exam to handle the sale. As you may imagine he had no idea of what to do. I contacted the title company and learned that we would need an affidavit from at least one heir who could attest to the fact that there were no more living heirs who might have a material interest in the property.

Somehow I found some paperwork with names of heirs and I began to search phonebooks. I found one possible lead in Williston Park, Long Island. To my astonishment I located someone who knew the family and was willing to sign the affidavit for me.

She was quite old and in ill health but thankfully her recall was excellent. Based on her input I composed an affidavit and drove her to a nearby drugstore where she signed it in front of a Notary Public.

When the title company received it, they rejected it because of some technicality in the wording. I had to retype the document, go back to Williston Park and drag this poor sick lady back to the drugstore again. Eventually I got it right and the sales process began in earnest.

Mom had slowly reconciled with the idea of saying goodbye to life as we had known it for more than a quarter of a century. We continued our search for a place to live, always with the same negative reaction by Mom. Eventually I took things into my own hands. I diligently examined advertisements and went out on inspections myself. My strategy finally paid off and not a moment too soon.

Chapter 58
End of an Era

By the time we sold the house our neighborhood was a total disaster area. It had become a haven for lowlifes, criminals and other miscreants. The alleys between the myriad apartment buildings that had provided us with great cover for "hide and seek" in the forties and fifties were now dark, clandestine passageways where heroin, marijuana, and LSD were routinely sold, and used. Addicts shot up and staggered out onto sidewalks once filled with my friends and me jumping rope, playing hopscotch, jacks, and box-ball.

Streets lined with bustling apartment dwellings and private homes, where we enjoyed stickball, kick the can, and Johnny on Pony were now covered with empty lots strewn with rubble and decaying skeletons of buildings abandoned by their owners, many of whom could not afford to keep up with repairs. Deserted buildings now framed the Major Degan and Cross Bronx Expressways like bombed out shells of WWII Berlin.

No doubt many factors contributed to the demise of the Bronx and other parts of the city. Many attribute much of it to the building of the Cross Bronx Expressway completed in 1963. Others, however, believe it was more likely the building of Co-op City, completed in 1969 in the northeast part of the borough that was *the* death knell to the Bronx.

This veritable city within a city became the largest cooperative housing development in the world with more than 15,000 residential units. As Yogi Berra would say, "it was déjà vu all over again." Like the Cross Bronx Expressway, it triggered yet another mass migration that emptied apartments, this time throughout the entire borough. Renters from all over including the Grand Concourse and Pelham Parkway, home to the more affluent residents in years gone by, saw an opportunity to own a new apartment at an attractive price. Again, the void created by the mass exodus resulted in further major population shifts.

This time Mom and I, the last of our neighbors and merchants to leave, joined the masses. In the spring of 1970 we closed the door of 1972 Daly Avenue behind us. Years later I visited; I drove around streets that now appeared much smaller than I remembered. My heart stopped at the sight of the empty lot where our house had stood since 1906. Only the two corner buildings remained.

It was then that I realized that Thomas Wolfe's "You Can't Go Home Again" could not apply more than it does to what was 1972 Daly Avenue, Bronx, New York.

Part VI
Eastward Bound

Chapter 59
Crossing the Bridge

Hundreds of golden forsythia blooms flashed a warm welcoming smile through the dinette window. The sun poured through the many windows of our freshly painted new home a short ride from the Queens side of the Throgs Neck Bridge. For a moment, Mom felt a little better about the move that had been so difficult for her to accept.

Our new dwelling in Bayside Queens was in some ways similar to the house. It was a garden apartment with a bit of an unusual twist. The two bedroom unit had a back entrance that faced an unused, fenced-in grassy area originally meant for tenants use but obviously ignored for many years.

As soon as the movers left, we transplanted a small rose bush that we had brought with us. Within weeks Mom and I cleaned out debris, turned the soil, and spread fertilizer. We planted a crab apple tree against a common garage wall, arranged beds of red and white impatiens, pink and yellow begonias, purple petunias, and other colorful flowers around the perimeter and covered the center with Kentucky Blue grass. Before long our back door opened to a charming little retreat which was a reasonable facsimile of the old homestead.

On the surface the community seemed like a perfect fit for us. Mom, who never drove, easily walked to a small shopping strip a block away on Frances Lewis Boulevard, a street not unlike Tremont Avenue, albeit much wider and busier. A large Waldbaum's supermarket at the corner of our street and the boulevard would supply most of our needs. A variety store and bank rounded out the convenient shopping strip. Two blocks in the other direction, there was also a Laundromat to which Mom could easily walk.

Mom again spent her leisure hours tending her garden tilling, planting and tending flowers as she had for the past twenty-six years. Neighbors passed as they went to and fro along a narrow pathway.

A once fallow enclosure turned into a colorful oasis somewhat similar to the one she nurtured in the Bronx albeit without the quiet privacy. All of a sudden neighbors, who never paid attention as they passed, began to occasionally use it for barbecues and social gatherings. They asked if it was OK and invited us to join them but we really didn't fit in.

It was clear that Mom was never really comfortable in this setting; we were out of place. The young families – most had lived there for many years and had children of similar age – were pleasant enough but neither Mom nor I shared any common ground with them. It was particularly hard on her, alone at home all day – no more Beck's farm – no more Grand Central Station. She missed her old life and friends. Shirley and I thought she needed more time and that she would eventually adjust and enjoy the calm, relatively safe atmosphere.

As for me, I spent very little time at home. I left for work every morning and came home late in the evening. In my off hours I was mobile and continued my social life with friends who now lived in Manhattan, Queens and Brooklyn.

Most important we were back in a working-middle-class neighborhood much like ours had been before it was so badly blighted. Despite Mom's misgivings she smiled when she saw kids playing in the street again; adults walking freely day or night. She worried less about me arriving home late at night and relaxed when she saw me park in front of our door without looking back over my shoulder.

The spring flowers that greeted us on our arrival were joined by a flourishing garden that seemed to hold promise for a brighter future.

Chapter 60
Gold Coast Calls

A few months after Mom and I relocated to Bayside the unique relationship that I had enjoyed with Marion for the past five years began to give way under the weight of the old proverb "all good things must come to an end."

Several conditions conspired to trigger its pending demise. At the crux was the transfer of our office from the home environment we shared, just the two of us, to a nearby commercial building. The company was growing as were our marketing efforts. At the same time a new office building was going up on 86th Street between Lexington and Third Avenues, just blocks from our home office. And, finally it didn't hurt that the landlord who was going to maintain offices in the building was drop dead gorgeous – a veritable combination of Gregory Peck, Cary Grant and Paul Newman. Rest assured all we did was look; Marion and he were both very married and I knew I didn't have a chance to get to know him better under any circumstances.

At first it was exciting. Marion and I were involved in everything from laying out the space to include private offices, a general office, conference room and a small presentation room with theater seats and the works. We selected warm wood flooring, modern furniture and state of the art equipment. We watched as the large empty space became an airy, attractive functional workspace.

Then we moved in, hired additional help and boom – everything changed. The biggest transformation was in how we each perceived what was going to happen. I naively thought that we would maintain our close relationship; she saw a large empire where I would be her henchwoman – a middle management position to which I never aspired – one which assigns responsibility for the behavior of others without power to reward or punish them – making meeting the objectives impossible to achieve.

To illustrate: Marion occupied the corner office while I worked in an adjacent one; both opened to the general office where several young ladies worked. When, on occasion, they engaged in conversation about their weekend, laughing out loud or talking on the phone, invariably my phone rang.

"Do you hear what's going on out there?" she would almost shout to which I replied yes.

"Well get out there and tell them to be quiet!" she commanded.

At first I did what I was told but then it occurred to me that she was just as close as I was and my job and title had nothing to do with disciplining anyone. I began to resent the change in my role. Other incidents occurred that were wearing on our once close relationship.

The straw that broke the camel's back was when she asked me to speak to Kathy, Mr. Grrrr's assistant from the ad agency, about joining us to assist me with my growing workload. I liked Kathy and we could use some extra help.

"Fine, what should I say if the subject of salary comes up?" I asked.

When she came back with a number greater than what I was earning I saw red. I didn't say anything. I passed the offer on to Kathy who turned it down cold. I, however, continued to be bothered by the incident and considered quitting. So, I updated my resume and then made a mortal mistake; I asked our crack typist who I thought was loyal to me to type it.

A few days later, I arrived to find Marion standing in my office. Fuming, she said.

"Are you looking for another job? After all this time – after all I've done for you, you're sneaking around preparing a resume to leave?" She gave me a little shove. I may have returned one. We exchanged more words and the next thing I knew I threw my keys on her desk and walked out.

I applied for unemployment and was turned down. The reason: "your employer said you left of your own accord." *What?* I called Marion:

"Are you telling unemployment that I left of my own accord?"

"Yes, I don't recall telling you to leave." Again, we had different perceptions of what took place. We proceeded to have a short conversation: she agreed to approve my request and we promised to stay in touch. That was our last conversation. I regret how I handled the situation. I should have talked to her about my hurt feelings; it is possible that she just wasn't thinking about my salary when telling me to make a higher offer to my potential assistant.

It bothered me to leave such a positive relationship on a negative note. I would like to say I learned from my behavior but I'm not sure how I would react to a similar situation today.

I will, however, always be grateful to Marion. For the third time in my career, I experienced one of life's ironies. Sometimes bad things actually turn into good ones: the first was when I was fired from the full-charge bookkeeping job for which I was ill-prepared that resulted in my introduction to the world of advertising; then I had Mr.Grrrr to thank for forcing me into the pivotal position from ad agency to the client side of the business, and finally this falling out with one of my greatest bosses who let me spread my wings and learn.

This time I really thought I did it; three strikes and your out. Lucky for me, the fourth time was the charm. Leaving Marion was the impetus for yet another career change that took me away from New York City to the Gold Coast of Long Island.

Chapter 61
Crowning a Career

For the first time in my working career, I drove seventeen miles to and from work instead of taking smelly subways and buses. Getting into my own car and driving to work had been a dream since I was five when my car was a cardboard box in a game of house.

It was the fall of 1970. We had settled into our new home. I had been searching for a new job for several months when I came upon an ad for a company located in Glen Cove, Long Island. I landed the job of *Assistant* Advertising manager, which, while seemingly a step backward from "Advertising Manager," was a big step forward.

Pall Corporation was a public company with sales of twenty-six million dollars compared to five million; the advertising budget too was some five times as large as Marion's. And, I was hired because the Advertising Manager needed help to deal with the rapid growth the company was beginning to experience that continued exponentially for the thirteen years I was employed there and beyond – today sales are over two billion dollars.

My new position offered me opportunities to be more creative – to write more, to be involved in design and production of a variety of communication media used to promote products for industrial and airplane hydraulic systems, pharmaceutical and chemical producers as well as biomedical applications. Even my bookkeeping experience came into play more as I oversaw larger campaigns and bigger budgets.

I played major roles in planning events like the annual meeting for stockholders as well as internal meetings with marketing and outside sales personnel; travelled more to set-up and work at trade shows and worked closely with top – and middle management professionals on a daily basis. The President was a brilliant, affable guy who made it his business to talk to everyone on a casual basis. The founder was a genius physicist who got his start in fine filtration while working on the Manhattan project, a research project that resulted in the development of the first nuclear weapons during World War II.

Our department expanded along with sales and expanding markets; we relocated to several different locations as work space became tighter. The last place I worked at was the old Woolworth Estate in Glen Cove., NY. It was one of several Gold Coast mansions with imported marble walls and floors, ornate gold-leafed cathedral ceilings with elaborate, crystal chandeliers and perfectly groomed gardens overlooking Long Island Sound, visible from my corner office windows.

The idea that people had lived like this was unbelievable to me, especially when you realize that Mr. Woolworth amassed his fortune from nickel and diming consumers in his chain of "five-and-ten cent" stores. They were an early version of variety stores like today's dollar stores.

According to Wikipedia, Mr. Woolworth opened his first store in Lancaster, Pa and his second with $127.50 in Harrisburg, the neck of the woods where Ben and family settled.

I marveled every morning as I, that kid from the Bronx, drove up the half mile meandering private road to my corner office. The mansion was one of several on the north shore of Nassau County known as the Cold Coast and made famous in the 1920s for its role as the backdrop in F. Scott Fitzgerald's classic novel, "Great Gatsby."

Although it was my place of employment, not my home I couldn't help but wonder from time-to-time: *How did I get here from there?*

Chapter 62
Better Times Prove Fleeting

In the spring of 1972, life was looking good. Mom's garden was flourishing she was somewhat at home in the neighborhood and, except for bouts with fatigue she seemed fairly healthy.

I was enjoying my job. The company closed between Christmas and New Years so I was going on two vacations a year. My friends and I took several trips up and down the east and west coasts of the U.S as well as Montreal and Quebec City in Canada.

A fly and drive vacation took us to Yosemite National Park for our first and only camping experience with outside bathroom facilities, followed by Lake Tahoe, San Francisco, the seventeen mile drive down the scenic pacific coast with stops at the Hearst Castle, Carmel, Santa Barbara, Disneyland and finally Los Angeles. We took the bus trip to gape at the gated homes of Hollywood stars and visited Universal Studios to learn how movies were made – a far cry from today's computer generated films.

I worried about leaving Mom alone on these outings but she encouraged it. Shirley kept a close watch on her from Central Islip and when a blizzard hit while I was in Caracas, Venezuela, Arnie walked four miles of snow covered, impassable roads to check on her. In the aftermath of that storm, when the doors opened at Kennedy Airport upon our arrival we, along with other passengers, hesitated to disembark and tried to negotiate a deal to stay on the plane for a return trip to warm, sunny South America.

The vacation that was to be the pièce de résistance was planned for the fall of 1972; it included Barcelona, Madrid, Lisbon, and four cities in North Africa – all in two weeks.

Since Elaine and I planned it without the benefit of a travel agent or the faintest idea of the region, we had a hectic agenda. We found ourselves in the air almost daily. Our trek started in Barcelona for a day or two; then we flew to Madrid. From there we were scheduled to take an afternoon flight to Casa Blanca. Although we were at the airport with plenty of time we missed our flight because we didn't understand the Spanish announcements. Luckily, I carried a schedule of all airline flights in our itinerary which, after some incomprehensible discourse, got us onto a late-night flight to our destination.

The Casa Blanca airport in the middle of the night looked like an outdoor mosque; we were greeted by a large number of men bowing down — not in deference to our arrival, but in prayer. We found a taxi and travelled in pitch blackness for about an hour to our hotel. We finally arrived exhausted, a bit frightened and relieved to have made it safely.

The next morning we rented a car with a standard transmission which only Sybil knew how to drive. The problem was that in short order she became too ill to leave the hotel room; the desk clerk recommended a doctor who gave her something for her ailing stomach. Elaine and I, our hearts set and visiting the casino, decided to try to drive. Even though I never mastered driving a standard transmission, I took the wheel.

I had limited success maneuvering through strange streets and mountain highways but we eventually made it to our destination — albeit driving in first gear most of the way.

Sybil soon recovered and for the next seven days we travelled around Morocco, through Fez, Rabat, Marrakesh — walking the markets, souks, and Kasbah's — stopping to take photos with a snake charmer who placed his snake around our necks. We visited bazaars and bought handcrafted carpets and other mementos.

Finally we made our way by ferry from Tangiers through the Strait of Gibraltar to Costa del Sol. After a few days visiting Gibraltar and resorts in southern Spain it was on to Lisbon, Portugal where we stayed in a quaint fishing village — watched a fisherman carefully weave his net and visited some historic sights. In the evening we checked out the casino where most guests were formally dressed for the occasion and the service was impeccable — I used my old boss Marion's winning system and left the roulette table with thirty-five dollars more than I came in with.

After this whirlwind trip we headed home, exhilarated and exhausted. When we disembarked at the airport, Shirley was waiting for us with Arnie. The instant I saw this curious combo I had a sinking feeling that something bad had happened.

Chapter 63
Mama Faces Life's Final Challenge

Shirley and Arnie, who it turned out, had spent lots of time together in the last few days explained to me that Mama was in Flushing Hospital. A few days before I was scheduled to return from my vacation she woke up, hemorrhaging from the rectum. Her first reaction was to call Arnie; she remembered he had checked on her in a snow storm when I was in Venezuela and he was the closest person who could help her. Fortunately, he was at home. He came immediately and took her to the emergency room at Flushing Hospital.

I had been more concerned about leaving Mama for this trip; it was so far away and she was a bit under the weather. She had never fully regained her strength after her surgery three years earlier; frequent fatigue and continued weight loss seemed to indicate further problems.

I had taken her to a highly recommended neighborhood doctor a week before my scheduled departure. She performed a fairly thorough exam and took blood tests. The results showed slight anemia. The doctor prescribed iron pills and assured me that she was not worried and that I could go on vacation as planned. Mama echoed the doctor's advice and urged me to go. I did so somewhat reluctantly.

"She's OK now," Shirley went on at the airport. "But after they stopped the bleeding they ran a series of tests and found something suspicious in her cecum."

"Her what?" I asked.

"It's a small sac between the small and large intestine," Arnie filled in.

"She needs surgery right away. We made the decision to put it off until you came home. We didn't want to call you and upset you since you were due back anyway," Shirley went on.

After the initial shock, on the way to the hospital, I began to reflect on the last few years; Mom's continuing malaise following her gall bladder surgery

— the fact that Dr. Booher was surprised when he didn't find cancer — was it hiding all that time or did he miss it?

I immediately thought that if it turned out to be cancer I wouldn't want her to be cared for in a local hospital with limited resources and a less than excellent reputation; the surgery should be done by specialists in a hospital that specializes in cancer. I tried to convince the rest of the family but they were taken by Dr. Schultz, the surgeon who had been so good during the emergency. I met with him and discussed my concerns. He urged me not to waste time and assured me that he would do a good job; I acquiesced.

The bowel resection was a success but the patient would soon die because it was cancer and it had metastasized to the liver. After a week of recovery we took Mama home and tried to pretend that the worst was over. But she had questions.

"Do I have cancer?"

"No, we said, you had a tumor in your intestines and it was removed."

"But was it cancer?"

"No," we lied.

Several of Mom's friends had succumbed to the disease. It was so dreaded at the time that many people of her generation could not utter the word. So how were we to tell her that she had it? We didn't. We established a policy of deny, deny, deny. We told everyone who came in contact with her to follow suit. I suspect that despite our denials she knew.

When she was able to travel, I took her back to the group of doctors who had operated on her gall bladder. They were well respected oncologists on the cutting edge of then very experimental chemotherapy treatment. Soon she started to experience temperature spikes; we tried experimental intensive chemotherapy. She was hospitalized and pumped full of chemicals that caused explosive vomiting, disorientation and general malaise. We tried to ply her with food despite her lack of appetite. She shrunk from her usual 157 pounds down to less than 90; eventually she became incontinent, often incoherent and ultimately prone to convulsions that accompanied wide spikes in temperature.

We obtained home health aides to care for her during the day. I continued to go to work; my employers were very understanding of the time I took off, late arrivals and frequent mid-day breaks to respond to concerns at home as well as darting out at five o'clock sharp in the evening. Shirley came from Central Islip to Bayside whenever she could. Toward the end Gerry frequently stayed overnight to help try to make Mama more comfortable, an impossible feat.

When she stopped visiting doctors, Mama was convinced that we had lied to her; that she had cancer and was dying. I spoke to Dr. Schultz and he came to visit her at home which seemed to give her temporary hope. I asked him:

"What can I give her to eat? She has no appetite. Can I try deli to whet her appetitive?"

"Are you kidding? At this point give her whatever the hell she wants!"

One evening I had to go into Manhattan to pick something up at the doctor's office. Standing at the elevator doors to leave – sleep deprived, aching for what Mama was going through and feeling totally helpless – I began to weep uncontrollably. One of the nurses passed by and beckoned me to her office. She put her hand on my shoulder and tried to console me.

"Maybe," she said you should consider putting your Mom into Calvary. Are you familiar with Calvary Hospital in the Bronx?"

"Never heard of it," I responded, tears streaming down my cheeks.

"It is a hospice; they have a wonderful way of dealing with end-of-life patients – no tubes and breathing devices; no heroic life-saving attempts. It is staffed by an order of nuns who help people die with dignity.

"So you're saying I should send my mother there to die. I don't think so."

"Why don't you take a look at it? If you decide to go ahead, just call me. We will have to fill out some paperwork. They only take patients with a life expectancy of less than twelve weeks."

The next night my best friend, Ann and I gathered the courage to visit Calvary. The first thing that struck me when we walked through this institution for the dying was the silence; there was no screaming and crying out in anguish that I had anticipated from visits to nursing homes. We glanced into several rooms –there were no artificial breathing sounds of ventilators, just patients sleeping peacefully.

The next morning I called the nurse back. She did the paperwork. I picked it up that night and two days later, her eyes wide with uncertainty, concern and terror, Mama was loaded into an ambulance en route to Calvary Hospital. I accompanied her; Gerry followed.

We did our best to comfort her but her greatest consolation came the moment she was in the hands of compassionate professionals. For the first time since her death journey began, Mama seemed somewhat at ease. I regretted that I hadn't known about Calvary sooner.

The last time I saw her was when I tiptoed into the dark, sterile, eerily still room. She woke from a rare peaceful sleep.

"Is that you Susie? What are you doing here so late?"

"I was just passing by so I thought I'd stop in to see how you are doing."

"I'm OK but now I'll worry about you getting home so late. Go home, I'm OK."

It was about 10:00PM, Sunday, May 6, 1973. Mama had been at Calvary for just three days; it was her penultimate destination nine months after her arduous final journey began.

When the phone rang twelve hours later at 10:00AM on May 7, I froze. Shirley had stayed over. She picked it up. Her face immediately confirmed my worst nightmare; I faintly heard the soft incoming voice coming through the phone:

"We're sorry to tell you that your mother passed peacefully in her sleep early this morning. Staff was with her at the time. Please contact a funeral home to make the necessary arrangements and come by at your convenience to pick up her personal belongings."

Just like that, it was over. Despite months of anxiety, frustration, our lives suspended on an emotional rollercoaster, Mama had slipped away. I stood dazed, shocked, speechless. Could Mama be gone? Could it be that this complex person, so much a part of me, was no more?

Even after I witnessed Dad instantly turn marionette-like, his head in my arms and heard the rattle of his last breath leave his being; even realizing for months that Mama's moment was imminent, the reality of it was incomprehensible. I didn't know what I felt.

For her I sensed relief; her pain, discomfort and terror had ended. For myself I experienced an enormous emptiness, and for this thing we call life, it brought back the issue of the inexplicable meaning of it all.

Just as it had when Dad died, the burning question returned: how could one who survived so much and so profoundly affected so many be snuffed out with such swiftness and finality, lost forever to those they touched.

Part VII
Moving Forward

Chapter 64
Lifelong Friendship to Partners for Life

At this writing, Arnie has been in my life for six decades. We met when he moved across the street; I was three months past my thirteenth birthday and he was busy preparing for his upcoming Bar Mitzvah in the fall of 1952.

He was already almost six feet tall with dirty blond hair and dreamy blue eyes . . . but who noticed. It feels like yesterday when I watched the new boy on the block walk past my house many nights on his way home at 10:00PM; when I took note of him sweeping Goretsky's drugstore floor at his after-school job, and when I snuck a glance while he hung out with his best friend Marty in front of his building.

After one look, Brenda stuffed sox into her bra and batted her eyes at him, but he wasn't quite ready for that. His friend Benny Goodman – not nearly as good looking, however, quickly responded with a bouquet of colorful flowers and a request for a movie date. That didn't go anywhere. She still introduces Arnie as her first boyfriend. Lots of girls in school had crushes on Arnie and he had a few of his own.

At fifteen my hormones went into gear and I had my first teen romance with Dickie McGee that lasted a few months. A short time later Tiny, nicknamed for his 6'2", 250 pound body, started showing up and we spent a lot of time together. It was then that our little group – Arnie, Marty, Roz and Tiny formed. We hung out together; usually on my stoop. At seventeen, Tiny who was a car buff, got his first jalopy; almost nightly we piled in and took to the roads.

In the next few years Tiny taught the female part of the group to drive and we bought our first partnership car.

Eventually I bought my own car and parked it in a parking lot around the corner. Arnie offered to chaperone me to and from this eerie, dark and deserted area. It was there that our platonic friendship began to turn. A first kiss led to another and another.

By then we had both graduated from high school. He was attending City College - Downtown and waiting to be called to military service. I was working. Although we mutually enjoyed each other's company, to say the least, we were not ready to go steady (the term used at the time to denote exclusivity) or make any long-term commitments.

Roz, who was also attracted to him, however felt that she was ready to settle down. Before I knew it they were together and over the next few months their relationship grew. In the fall of 1959 he pushed up his draft and was off to the Fort Jackson Army base in South Carolina for basic training. The separation was too much for them so in May, 1960 they were married; she had just turned twenty-one and he would do so in September.

We all remained friends; there were no hard feelings. The genuine friendship between Arnie and me was once again purely platonic. I would not have considered marriage to him or anyone else at the time. I was enjoying making my own money and new found independence. I imagined and hoped for a more affluent future – perhaps a professional companion, travel and security.

By March 1961 Arnie and Roz became the proud parents of Mark. Arnie was assigned to the finance department at Camp Kilmer, New Jersey. After his discharge in the winter of 1962, they moved to a new project in Staten Island; many of their neighbors were, like them, young families just starting out. They bonded and established a fun social life.

On the strength of his financial management experience in the Army, Arnie landed a responsible position in a large, well established Wall Street brokerage firm; his job was to obtain and manage short-term loans of tens of millions of dollars to provide day-to-day working capital.

It didn't take long before he developed a strong distaste for the politics and back-stabbing atmosphere on Wall Street. As a kid he had always thought he wanted to be a doctor or a policeman. So when he became aware that a police exam was coming up he took it, passed it and was placed on a waiting list.

While he waited to be called, he left Wall Street and tried his hand at insurance sales with Equitable Life Insurance. He was able to make a living at it for a few years but couldn't wait to enter the Police Academy. That finally happened in 1965.

Soon after his appointment, in February of 1966, Robin came along. Everyone was overjoyed with the new addition. Roz had her hands full as a full time homemaker with two small children and Arnie was in a career that he had dreamed of when he was a kid.

For his first seven years as a Patrolman he worked around the clock in shifts from 8AM to 4PM, 4-12AM and 12AM to 8AM; he walked a beat in Brooklyn, found himself on patrol in the thick of the race riots of the late 1960s, and handled calls ranging from delivering a baby-to- saving a man choking on his own regurgitation-to-subduing a mentally debilitated drunk who stabbed his aging aunt to death after he was released from the mental wars of the hospital the next day.

In 1967 he was promoted to Sergeant and assigned to the Organized Crime Control Bureau where he supervised a team of detectives. Under the then Mayor Beam, they worked to rid the city of crimes perpetrated by organized crime families from internal murders-to gambling, and sexually illicit establishments, all of which are the stuff of exciting movies and TV shows. They also provided fodder for many titillating and nail-biting tales told to friends and family as only Arnie can tell them.

Somewhere along the way, as often happens, Arnie and Roz grew apart; after twelve years of trying to keep it together, they separated. Late in 1972, Arnie took a small apartment nearby and they were legally separated. He remained close to Mark and Robin, geographically, emotionally, and in every way possible before and after the divorce became final early in 1974.

I know that if there were any way he could have stayed in the marriage, if just for the sake of the children he loves so much, Arnie would have; his continuing attentiveness bears this out.

Unlike many men who divorce their children along with their wives, Arnie remained connected and has been there for his kids – and Roz as well, for which I have always respected him.

While my dear friends were experiencing a domestic meltdown, I too went through some difficult times, the worst of which were nursing both my parents through long debilitating illness that ended in death. And, while I enjoyed life I had not found that ideal companion to share it with.

We commiserated with and comforted each other throughout the years. In our mid-thirties, an undercurrent of chemistry that had been submerged for a dozen years – through life experience, ups and downs, mutual caring and compassion – slowly resurfaced and reawakened feelings we'd had for each other in our youth.

Our on-again, off-again platonic relationship was off again - this time replaced with a lifetime commitment.

Chapter 65
Marrying a Family

It seemed almost prophetic, as if we were meant to be bound in marriage. While I loved Arnie and wanted the best possible outcome for Mark and Robin, the decision to marry a whole family was quite difficult. Questions whirled. Stepfamilies are usually a challenge under the best circumstances. And this was about as far as you could get from the "best."

In the end we decided that no matter how counter-intuitive it seemed, our love, friendship and shared values would see us through. And strange as it sounded, it could be good for the kids, and yes, even Roz in the long run.

To avoid adding trauma or pouring salt on any wounds, we exchanged wedding vows on January 30, 1975, a cold rainy evening at a neighborhood synagogue. In attendance were just the two of us, the Rabbi and ten old men (the number required for a minion to make it official). They held up the Chupa, the ritual canopy that represents a welcoming home the couple will establish together.

On the way to the ceremony we stopped at the photographer's studio and posed for a photo to mark the occasion. In our desire to cause as little disruption as possible, we ruffled a few feathers of family and friends who felt they should be a part of our wedding celebration.

Afterward we enjoyed a quiet dinner and a weekend away in Pennsylvania Dutch country. And, on Monday morning we were back at work.

So began a major adjustment for everyone. We faced many of the usual stepfamily problems. The kids had to overcome conflicts of loyalties between their parents, as well as me. Questions of authority take on new perspectives: "You can't tell me what to do, you're not my mother," soon becomes a familiar refrain.

The title of "stepmother" carries with it the wicked "Cinderella" stigma as well. The term originally referred to "one who steps in to care for children who lose a parent." In my case, and I'm sure with the increase in blended families, it doesn't feel entirely accurate. I think "other mother" may be more appropriate.

Semantics aside, I quickly learned that one needs the "wisdom of Solomon," the self-confidence of a Donald Trump whose name adorns his vast empire of real estate and the hard shell of a tortoise to survive. You must accept that you do not share the unconditional, almost indestructible love that flows from the biological parent-child relationship regardless of the quality of that relationship.

We briefly entertained the thought of having children together, but rejected the idea for many reasons; to avoid creating jealousies was high on the list. Others had to do with finances — we needed two incomes to maintain two households. Besides, being a biological mother was never a high priority for me. After experiencing a difficult childhood I didn't have a driving desire to bring others into this world to face similar challenges. Luckily, Mark and Robin fulfilled Arnie's desire for a family so I was off the hook.

That didn't mean I didn't enjoy having Robin spend weekends and holidays with us. Prior to our marriage she had frequently visited. We continued to go to the park, the beach and Adventurer's Inn in Whitestone, Queens. One month after we married, for her ninth birthday we bought her a beautiful pink (she remembers yellow) Schwinn bicycle with a banana seat and the three of us often rode together in a nearby park.

As for Mark, six-feet tall at the age of fourteen, he moved in with us within the first few months of our marriage. He attended high school in Bayside which was the highest rated school district in Queens.

Within the first six months we started house hunting. We couldn't afford much but we wanted our own private home. Our primary criteria were limited: 1) that the house had to be close to the Flushing apartment where the kids lived with their Mom much of the time 2) that it be detached and 3) that it have at minimum a private driveway and 4) it had to be priced so that our total savings of $12,000 covered the required 20% down payment and closing costs. Not much to ask for. After a year of looking at houses we ran across an ad in Newsday that met those bare requirements.

Although the fifty-year-old Dutch Colonial was situated a half block from the Long Island Expressway and some of our closest neighbors included a gas station, restaurant and house of worship, we bought it and it served us well.

Benjamin Cardozo, the best high school in the five boroughs was around the corner as was Queensborough Community College. Both Mark and Robin attended the high school. At sixteen, however, Mark was off to a military school in Florida. After graduation he worked in the Daytona area for a short while before returning to New York where he lived with his Mom and enrolled at Queensborough to pursue an AAS degree in Business Administration.

Robin and I continued to bond – I helped her with her homework, together we picked Cheeta, our family pet, from all the adorable kittens at North Shore Animal League. When we shopped for her clothing she barred me from the dressing room; at times I felt this was indicative of her difficulty to fully let me into her life.

Over time, somehow, with sensitivity, understanding and more than a few bruised egos, our little family unit overcame many step-related problems. We grew together. I learned to accept my quasi parent-child role. Mark and Robin slowly accepted that, their luck, they had to deal with two mother figures. In time, they grew up and we grew older.

In October 1988, Robin married Glenn. It was the first time Roz and I met face to face. As we prepared for the ceremony in the dressing room, she approached me:

"Hi, I want to thank you for all you've done for the kids, especially Robin over the years and everything you did to make this day so perfect."

"It was my pleasure," I assured her.

With that simple exchange the iceberg that had characterized our relationship dissolved and we became friends again. Growing up, Roz always made me laugh more than anyone else. She began joining us for holiday dinners, family celebrations and casual gatherings. When the grandchildren were born we rejoiced together. We celebrated every birthday and milestone together along with Mark, (and for many years, his ex-wife Connie), as well as Glenn's Mom, Miriam, his brother, Neil, sister-in-law, Bonnie and niece, Amanda.

I like to think Arnie was right; in many ways our marriage was beneficial for everyone involved. Perhaps, I gained more than anyone else. How else would I have enjoyed the role of parenting without the labor pains; become a grandmother to Adam and Jenna and taken such pleasure in being part of their lives, living next door, and watching them grow into terrific caring adults, not to mention being grandma to Lexi, our beloved granddog who unfortunately after nine and a half years of making us smile with her antics succumbed to a long illness in late spring 2012.

Roz, too, reaped the benefits of friendship and family. We were there for her whenever she needed help. She always felt free to call Arnie who immediately responded no matter the time of day or night when she suffered an attack of Ménière's disease that was marked by episodes of vertigo, severe dizziness, nausea, and vomiting which often left her incapacitated and frightened for hours and sometimes days at a time. She also counted on us when dealing with complications of diabetes and its many problems. Finally, after she was diagnosed with late-stage lung cancer and spent the last year of her life in a nursing home near our home, we visited her regularly and were at her beck and call. We lost her ten days before her sixty-fourth birthday and I miss her.

I have always been a bit of a fatalist and can't help but wonder about how things worked out. Had any event single gone differently in either of our lives, in all likelihood, the love, respect and mutual caring Arnie, *the family* and I have shared for almost thirty-eight years, and counting, would have remained submerged forever.

Chapter 66
New Home Stirs Old and New-Found Memories

Our aluminum clad colonial, turned a dirty mustard color with time, sat on a 35' x 100' foot lot separated from our neighbors on either side by a single car-width driveway on a block zoned for mixed residential and commercial use. 220th Street in the Oakland Gardens section of Bayside was a narrow street that routinely served as a detour for a main shopping area one block east. It was divided by the Long Island Expressway (LIE) a half-block from our home.

After a year of house hunting every weekend we were so happy to find a place we could afford that met our basic needs, we closed our eyes to the corner gas station, heavy traffic as well as the noise and air pollution spewed by the LIE. A forty-foot tall blue spruce tree concealed the entire house from the outside and the street from the inside.

On the morning of October 1, 1976 I dug up the rosebush that Mom and I had transported from the Bronx and followed the moving van to our "new" house. The living quarters were typical of homes built fifty years earlier. Though smaller than we would have liked, they offered more space than we had in the apartment. What's more, it also had old-world charm — high ceilings, curved archways, moldings and an original built-in working fireplace.

The next morning we sat in the tiny breakfast nook at the old oak table which, along with two chairs, barely fit. As we gazed out the window we discovered an unexpected bonus: our back yard, which we had only given a cursory look before, was much more secluded, tranquil and country-like than we had imagined.

A low, wide-spread canopy of lucent green, tri-lobed leaves on two thirty-foot tall maple trees, one in each far corner, were accompanied by myriad rose bushes, hydrangeas, lilacs and other foliage enveloping us in a cocoon of privacy. The leaves of the twin trees gently brushed against each other and draped over the top of the six-foot ivy covered stockade fence across the back of the narrow yard.

The soaring maple sentries, probably planted soon after the house was built in 1926, became the root of many pleasurable and memorable moments. In summer, they offered shade for family and friends to play, read, or just relax in comfort. They reduced the temperature behind the house which was always cooler than it was in front. In fall we were welcomed by a medley of hues – shades of russet, amber, gold. In winter snow fell on their nascent branches to create a magnificent wonderland of white lace.

Years later we had the trees pruned at the request of a neighbor seeking more sun. The pruner sized up the situation, tied himself – first to one and then the other – and systematically removed branch after branch. As each limb fell so did my heart.

Every succeeding year brought less foliage. The trunk and branches soon began to dry out. Eventually they died and we had them taken down. Suddenly we became very aware that we did indeed live in the city. The six-foot fence and shrubs became impotent, without the help of the trees, to camouflage the urban-like structures a stone's throw away, or to provide the intimacy that we had enjoyed. The hot sun beat down on visitors during the summer. The fall color display and the tranquil scenes of winter were gone.

Even then, however, our maple sentries continued to fuel many a roaring fire on a cold winter night. Sometimes when I gazed into the flames I saw them standing tall over memorable moments in the backyard they had protected for so many years.

One of the most vivid of the backyard recollections was a visit with Ben's family in the late '70s. While I recall get-togethers in both New York and Pennsylvania with Ben and his family throughout previous years, this one was the first time at our new home.

When we were still in the Bronx I remember taking the kids to Bronx Park and one unforgettable trip on Circle Line cruise around the city; Lynn looked like a miniature Debbi Reynolds with her beautiful blond hair, big blue eyes and bashful smile.

But Thanksgiving weekend at our house in Bayside stands out. We barbecued in the backyard. Ben, Doris, Ned with his wife, Brenda, daughter Jenny, son Noah, Brad and Ross slept on mattresses and innersprings laid out on floors all over the house. Lynn joined us later; Ben and Arnie picked her up at Kennedy airport from a band trip to Germany.

On Thanksgiving Day, the young Beck clan took in the sights in Manhattan; Arnie babysat eight-month-old Noah who fell asleep on his chest while I prepared Turkey dinner with all the trimmings. Mark and Robin finally met my family; Robin and Lynn, both fourteen, spent time some teen time comparing notes – everyone genuinely enjoyed the all-to-rare family togetherness – Cheeta, not so much – she spent the entire weekend under a bed, hiding from Jenny's enthusiastic arrival and discovery that we had a cat, a finding that probably cut short Cheeta's nine lives.

She did leave us in 1985. Two years later we adopted Nuggie and Smokie. Together they were our last pets and their antics are among the most cherished memories of our home of twenty five years in Bayside.

Chapter 67
Family Reunions, Best and Worst

Though my nuclear and now expanded extended family had not seen each other for many years before the 1977 Bayside reunion, it just so happened that, in the summer of 1978 we all met again at Shirley's farm in New Market Tennessee for a long weekend. Again, we had a grand time and as always we promised to maintain these important and joyful times together more often.

That did not come to pass. Arnie and I, however, visited both families on the way to and from vacations in Washington, DC and Hilton Head, South Carolina. Benny came up to New York a few times to attend Kirby Vacuum Cleaner conventions and stayed with us on those occasions.

Besides these infrequent face-to-face contacts, we stayed in touch by phone. Shirley and I spoke almost nightly and we both called Benny (he had an aversion to the telephone) and kept up with family comings and goings — military enlistments, marriages, births — most noteworthy events that make up life.

Unfortunately many of our later trips to Tennessee were for heartbreaking occurrences. In 1990 Gerry unexpectedly passed away from a heart attack or stroke; he died suddenly at home and the specific cause was never determined.

Then in 1999 Shirley became ill. When we spoke on the phone she coughed incessantly and told me she was spending lots of time in bed. She refused to see a doctor until some time in August when a friend insisted on taking her to the hospital. She was diagnosed with stage-four lung Cancer. That same evening while trying to stand up from a sitting position her left arm broke — the malignancy had metastasized to her bones.

We drove the 800 mile trip bi-weekly; in most cases we picked Benny up on the way. Sadly, it took a tragedy of this magnitude for us to spend more time together than we had throughout most of our adult lives. Shirley's arduous, devastating battle ended on December 8, 1999. We stayed in touch with

Neil, Julie and Margo but soon snapped back to very little contact which is now reduced to birthday and holiday greetings to Margo.

Neil married and moved to Iowa. Julie, her companion Jimmy and Margo continue to live at the family home in New Market. Arnie and I visited once to celebrate Margo's ninth birthday (she's now about to turn 24).

I continued to try to keep track of Ben and the family. Things were OK until, as they say, they weren't. Within a few years of Shirley's passing, Ben was diagnosed with Bladder Cancer. He had been making routine visits to the Veteran Administration facility for years where he was treated for a serious diabetes condition as well as cardiac follow-up following open heart surgery at age sixty-five.

We visited him when he was hospitalized at the VA hospital for short periods. On one visit he waited for us outside. I was taken aback and commented to Arnie:

"If I didn't know better I'd swear that was Mama sitting there."

"Wow," he responded, "the resemblance is uncanny."

He continued to be treated for about three years, continuously resisting seeing private doctors. By early 2004 his hospitalizations increased. Then, like Shirley, he too went to a nursing home. Again, Arnie and I visited frequently. Once more calamity brought us together with family, this time Doris and the kids. In his pain and anguish, my big brother felt sorry for me:

"Too bad you have to go through this," he said, "watching the family die one-by-one."

Soon after that, in June 2004 he passed away.

Three short months later Ned found Doris, who had a history of high blood pressure, dead in her bed apparently having passed quietly in her sleep.

With each loss there was one less person to reminisce with, to laugh with about our parents or our pasts, or to count on to ask questions that only family can answer, until there are none.

Even at my age this reality is hard to come to grips with. How often I wish I could still pick up the phone, visit with and host my family and friends who have been silenced by the nature of our mortal existence.

I once read a quote, the essence of which has been attributed to a Danish philosopher, Soren Kierkegard:

"Unfortunately we live life forward and understand it backwards."

Had I genuinely understood the finality and loneliness of life after losing those close to us perhaps I would have paid more attention.

Chapter 68
Car Careens into Arnie, Impacts My Career

Two major events conspired to expedite my unplanned early retirement: one a near catastrophe that had the potential to change our lives indefinitely; the other, less dramatic, yet life-altering.

On July 14, 1983, as I cleared my desk at about 5:30PM, my phone rang. It was Mark who never called me at work before. My heart stopped.

"Hello," he said, "Dad was hit by a car. We're at Long Island Jewish Hospital. You better come as soon as you can."

Shocked and dumbfounded, I asked,

"When, where, is he OK?"

"A car came up on the sidewalk on Bell Boulevard and hit him when he was walking on the overpass of the LIE on his way to the hardware store on the corner."

"Is he OK? Is he conscious?" I managed to ask.

"He's in and out."

My mind's eye immediately envisioned him near death or paralyzed for life.

I rushed out only to crawl through mid-July, Friday evening traffic. Cars and trucks jammed the LIE. I tried the parkway which wasn't much better. I jumped from one highway to another, then to local streets, tried to weave through what seemed like rows of stationary vehicles, all the time unable to erase the dreadful slide show that played over and over in my head.

When I finally arrived at the Emergency Room Arnie was conscious, he recognized me, smiled and said:

"I think my leg is broken, what happened?"

"You were hit by a car while you were walking on Bell Boulevard."

"How did that happen? Was I crossing the street?" I passed on what I had learned:

"An elderly woman on the way to the hospital for cancer treatment lost control of her car and mounted the sidewalk and hit you from behind."

"I think my leg is broken, what happened?" he repeated the question and would continue to do so for the rest of the night.

The medical team ran tests for brain damage; it turned out to be a concussion that would likely heal.

Several of his coworkers arrived at the hospital when they heard through the NYPD grapevine that one of their own had been hit. Robin and a friend came running in. We waited until the early morning hours, talking to Arnie — answering his repetitive questions over and over.

Then we listened to the drill as a rod was driven through his left calf as an anchor for the ropes that would hold his leg in traction for the next week until his erratic vital signs stabilized and surgery could be done on what turned out to be a badly broken femur.

It would take a week of uncertainty before we knew that he hadn't suffered brain damage. Then came the operation, in which they inserted a metal rod through his thigh bone from hip to knee and clamped a butterfly segment that had broken away in place.

The surgery was deemed a success. However, he woke in severe pain which persisted and was only somewhat relieved by strong pain killers. One week after surgery we brought him home. Still, he continued to endure acute pain and was dependant on crutches except for going up and down the stairs when he used his arms to lift himself backwards, sitting on his butt each step of the way. It was almost impossible for him to prepare meals, transport plates or anything else we carry through a day and take for granted when everything is in working order.

Mark and Robin were off from school, he from classes at Queensborough Community College and she waiting to enter her senior year in high school; they kept him company and provided tender love and care as needed while I continued to work and cover the early morning hours and evening TLC shifts.

It was difficult to leave him in that condition. It also happened to be at a time when I was increasingly unhappy at work. My boss with whom I thought I had an honest, warm, mutually respectful working relationship metamorphosed into someone I no longer recognized.

In response to explosive growth that triggered an expanding workload we reorganized the advertising department of two to the Marketing Communications Department. Each of the four distinct product lines serving aircraft, industrial, chemical processing and biomedical applications was assigned its own Manager. The Director handled "corporate communications" and oversaw all activity and we hired more support staff.

In addition, we also hired a departmental Production Manager from J. Walter Thompson, a large well-known ad agency in the city; his job was to take some of the burden off of the Managers and optimize efficiency. He would obtain multiple estimates to ensure optimum pricing, help select the right vendor for the job, and follow through to delivery and billing. These were all functions that took precious time away from the creative and administrative functions for which the managers were responsible.

Instead the new Production Manager completely changed the working dynamic; he immediately took full control from the Managers – replaced long-time, loyal and accommodating vendors, and most important failed to improve quality or reduce production costs.

When confronted by complaints from us, our boss insisted he had to back his new man. It didn't take long to smell a rat. I, and others, felt we were between the proverbial "rock and a hard place," suspecting something was terribly wrong but unable to talk to anyone about it without being disloyal to our boss who was likely a major player.

I tried to put my head in the sand, my nose to the grindstone and go about my own business hoping somehow things would change.

On a morning when I was particularly overwrought with Arnie's constant suffering at home and mine at the office, my boss caught me on the way into the office.

"Just want to give you a heads-up," he announced. "Eric (the Director of Human Resources who happened to be the son of the President) is going to be more involved with our department. He's going to have a desk here and observe us for a while."

It just felt like the last straw. Without putting my brain in gear, I blurted:
"You know what, that's it, I quit."

I don't know who was more shocked – he or I. He tried to belittle the new development,
"It won't be that bad. Calm down," he urged.

But once the words were out of my mouth, nothing could change my mind. I realized I really had had enough.

Besides, soon the kids would have to go back in school and Arnie, still not making the progress that was anticipated, would need help at home.

I offered my two weeks notice then and there and it was rejected. We talked a little more and negotiated a month's notice. I wrapped up my projects and passed the baton to my talented young assistant.

The evening before my last day my coworkers threw me a festive farewell party attended by inter-departmental co-workers, vendors; even Dr. Pall showed up. He was a shy retiring science genius who rarely socialized with employees. The primary reason he knew me, aside from occasional meetings, was that I was responsible for the production of a handsome leather-bound book containing engravings of his seventy-plus patent certifications presented to him at a celebration of the company's fiftieth anniversary.

He was very moved by this impressive tome, complete with biographical data written in gold and black calligraphy throughout. He was so impressed that he not only attended my party, he also extended an invitation to come back whenever I so desired.

That day would never come. Arnie was getting worse instead of better. We had to go back and forth to doctors more often. We went back to Dr. Schultz, Mom's doctor. He took and x-ray and said in his inimitable way.

"That's not bone, that's shit. You have a non-union. You are not healing and will not without more surgery."

My friend Laura happened to live next door to an orthopedic surgeon who worked at Columbia Presbyterian. We saw him and he agreed to replace the rod.

Arnie had also just received a congratulatory announcement of his promotion to Lieutenant. The ceremony would take place before the upcoming surgery and by this time the pain was almost constant and he could hardly walk. The doctor fitted him with a brace that went over his entire leg from hip to ankle. At the promotion ceremony the Police Commissioner was somewhat taken aback as he watched a stiff-legged, smiling soon to be promoted Sergeant, walk across the stage. He too smiled, shook his hand and congratulated Arnie as he presented him with his Lieutenant's shield.

During this difficult time, I gave little thought to working. One day I received a call from one of my ex-colleagues.

"They got 'em!" he whispered, a note of excitement and conspiracy in his voice.

"That's why Eric was hanging around – to confirm the kickback scheme that came to light in a covert investigation that was underway for some time. The indictments came in today; the two defendants were charged with embezzling hundreds of thousands of dollars. I knew it, he said triumphantly."

I didn't share my friend's enthusiasm. In one way I felt somewhat vindicated, I had been right and was glad I got out when I did; in another, however, I was hurt and disappointed – my feelings of affection and respect for my boss of thirteen years had been violated.

In the end, the two co-conspirators were found guilty, received a slap on the wrist and were forced to make restitution for a portion of the stolen funds. I always wonder if they regretted risking and losing their good positions, generous remuneration and above all their self-respect.

The first week of January 1984 Arnie underwent the second surgery to replace the rod in his femur and the pain he had lived with for six months vanished. Two weeks later he was back at work, this time in the Chief of Detectives Office in lower Manhattan. He had escaped relatively unscathed from what could have been a tragedy.

While on the mend he managed to take and pass the New York Bar exam, having graduated from Brooklyn Law School the month before the accident.

As for me, I found myself in an unintended retirement for which I was totally unprepared. The last six months had left me disillusioned – with what happened to Arnie and my own disappointing experience – what would come next? For some time, even before my dream career came to an abrupt halt, I had been thinking about doing something more meaningful – something with more socially redeeming value – with my life.

After seeing up close and personal, the uncertainties of life, perhaps it was time to try to turn near calamity into a new opportunity.

Chapter 69
Search for Meaningful Encore

"Far and away the best prize that life offers is the chance to work hard at work worth doing."
Theodore Roosevelt, *Speech in New York, September 7, 1903*

Almost thirty years after I first entered the workforce, experienced and with the luxury of not being under the gun to work to live, perhaps I would "work at work worth doing." While Arnie recuperated, I read and followed the guidelines of "What Color is Your Parachute," a popular guide for career changers that is still periodically updated.

For the first time in my life I felt like I actually had choices. Until my career abruptly ended I had been swept along a circuitous path; one thing just seemed to lead to another. I started to work days after I graduated from high school with no plan, no idea of what I wanted or would be able to do; I went into the world with the simple realization and resolution to work to somehow make a better life than the only one I knew.

The career guide recommends an exhaustive exploration of one's personal and professional assets, liabilities, likes, dislikes all of which I diligently wrote on 3" x 5" index cards that I carefully evaluated.

Then I did what I usually do; I decided to try something totally unrelated. I tend to over-think and examine every aspect of a decision – whether it's an investment, a purchase of anything from a camera to a house, or a vacation itinerary – then, and only then, do I make an impromptu choice that has absolutely nothing to do with my painstaking analysis.

In this case, during a casual conversation with a vendor with whom I had worked for a long time, he suggested I try my hand at commercial real estate brokerage.

"You'd be great at it and there's lots of money to be made," he said.

Hmm; counterintuitive as it sounded, money could account for lots of socially redeeming accomplishments. The requirements for a successful broker seemed to match my skills and experience. One had to have the ability to bring people together for the purpose of concluding a deal. Hell, as an advertising manager for all those years, I constantly acted as a broker between marketing, sales, top management and vendors to produce ads, literature, trade show exhibits — every element required in a productive marketing mix. It was not an easy task — every person involved had to sign off on each project. Each put his personal mark on it and they often conflicted with each other.

Why not give it a try, I thought. My vendor friend referred me to the broker who found him his space. We talked and in January 1984 I took to the retail centers, office buildings and industrial parks of Long Island with a Real Estate Salesperson license in hand. It was an exhilarating experience, learning the ins and outs of the business. I caught on quickly and leased my first office by March, which was some kind of record.

I checked ads, canvassed on the phone, drove around unfamiliar roads with my trusty maps, and dictated into a tape recorder any and all possible leads I could muster.

In the meantime, my twenty-eight year-old boss was brokering big deals for apartment buildings all over the city where the new co-op trend was hot; he was making a fortune. Landlords saw an opportunity to unload apartment buildings to young entrepreneurs who sold them in cooperative shares to existing tenants, renters turned apartment owners and investors. Co-ops were an excellent passive investment for professionals.

I convinced my broker to allow me to become involved and learned about investment real estate. We had a nice relationship with one exception; he had some trouble playing with others. He tended to cut into each salesperson's commissions. Admittedly he was a natural salesman and was quite helpful in closing deals; the problem was his half of the commission was supposed to cover that. He saw it differently and slashed our commissions based on the amount of time he put in on our deals. So, after one year I struck out on my own.

There was a slight glitch; I wasn't a broker and only a broker can operate a real estate business in New York State. To become one, a licensed salesperson must have executed a reasonable number of deals, completed a requisite number of required continuing education courses and take the "Broker's" test. I met the first two prerequisites but had to take the Broker's course and pass the mandatory test.

While I prepared, I worked feverishly from home to cement relationships, find listings and develop business. I quickly received my license and tried to get the business going. It soon became apparent that I may have left the nest too soon; I hadn't built enough loyal client relationships and despite my experience and negotiation skills I wasn't the best fit for this rough and tumble enterprise. Still, I forged ahead. A few of Arnie's co-workers joined me as salespeople. My friend Ann also came aboard to help search for listings.

Then, within our first year Uncle Sam changed the investment real estate rules – doctors, lawyers and other large investors who had seen a gold mine in passive investments could no longer benefit from them – they had to be actively engaged in the operation of their properties to take lucrative tax deductions. Puff went the real estate bubble. I, along with many others trying to go along for the ride, was out if business.

For a while I went back to commercial sales and leasing, working for another broker. It was a slow tedious process but I was in for the long haul – that was until October 1987 when Wall Street crashed. Clients with whom I had appointments called to cancel. For the next several months businesses decided to stay put until things came back to normal.

By the end of the year I was referring back to my self evaluation index cards for a new direction. The job market was still poor.

I decided to take a break from the business world and try free-lance writing – which I did with limited success for about six months. What I mean by limited success is that I received some very cordial, constructive rejections and was almost published – the keyword being "almost."

Once my creative juices were primed I went on to try oil painting. We had been searching for still-life art for our walls for some time. Why not paint my own? I located a great little place – a storefront, five minutes from home, in which the National Art League held classes for a small fee. The instructor was a retired commercial artist named Al. He walked around and helped each of the six or seven attendees individually.

At the first meeting he gave me a quick course on mixing colors, told me what to purchase and invited me back. I enjoyed going there for the next several months. With Al's help I painted a series of land- and seascapes depicting the four seasons – a few of which I gave to friends. Two food-oriented oil paintings adorn my dining room. I captured our two cats in oil. And, I was able to complete something Arnie had wanted and couldn't find, a painting of the Ten Commandments written out in English. I gave it to him as a birthday gift in 1987 and it hangs in a prominent place in our den.

While my paintings were passable, especially to those who love me, I recognized that it was just one more thing that, at best, I was mediocre at. My work was stiff and photography-like. Rather than feed my creative need, it confirmed that while I do have some graphic skills they are not those of a truly creative artist.

More important, I still felt that gnawing need to be productive, to contribute to society in some way. So I went back to school and completed a Master of Communication Arts degree program in the hope of transferring my marketing communication and writing skills perhaps to the non-profit sector.

Again, I managed to go in a different direction. This time to a short stint as an Adjunct Professor, teaching Advertising, Public Relations and Sales Promotion at the New York Institute of Technology, the institution from which I received my advanced degree. After spending so many years as a student I thought, "no problem, I can do this" only to find that the perspective from the other side of the desk was quite different. I had also been away from the business for some time by then and the world was rapidly changing.

The internet, referred to in the early 90's as the superhighway, was just getting underway and had begun to alter the way everything was done. Worse, I was shocked to find the world of academia extremely politically charged. I put my all into it for three semesters. Then one night, during a terrible winter storm, I received an offer to teach a late-night class in Manhattan. I turned it down and went back to the drawing board.

In the meantime Arnie's career in the police department continued to advance. By the late 1980's he was the second in command in his department at the Chief of Detectives Office. Word went out about the pending retirement of the Commanding Officer of the Detective Squad in Flushing, Queens just minutes from our home. Arnie was offered the position along with a promotion to "Lieutenant Commander." It was an excellent opportunity – not only prestigious but close to home with a nice salary bump to Captain's pay.

For the next seven years Arnie was in charge of the active detective squad, investigating cases from felonious assaults, kidnappings, rapes and armed robberies to gruesome mass murders. It wasn't unusual for him to be awakened in the middle of the night and work through several days to solve a case while the leads remained hot.

His high profile assignment got him on TV and in newspapers from time to time and rounded out a full, successful and distinguished thirty-one year career that ended with his retirement in 1995.

Consequently we were now both no longer working and at home together at the ripe old age of fifty-five. That required an adjustment. After a short period we took several trips by air, land and sea to Europe, the Bahamas, the Caribbean and around the country.

We also had the opportunity to spend lots of time with the children and grandchildren and most important each other, for which I am grateful. I am also thankful that to the best of my knowledge I am relatively healthy and able to function as I always have – so as I try to balance my good fortunes, I keep my eyes and ears open in my quest for what T. Roosevelt referred to as "work worth doing."

As a result, in the late nineties I volunteered in the literacy program at the Queens Public Library; after a training program given on five consecutive Saturdays I was assigned to the library in Jamaica Queens. As a general rule it is a one-on-one program – one tutor to one student. I, however, had witnessed a rare group session during one of our training sessions and mentioned it to the trainer:

"I noticed that there is a group session going on and it looks like everyone is very engaged and they seem to be enjoying themselves."

"That's an interesting observation," she said. "We only have that here in Jamaica because we have more people in need here."

You guessed it – I was assigned to tutor a group of five students: three immigrants from Guyana who had never attended school, a young man with traumatic brain injury and a middle-aged woman who grew up in Brooklyn, attended high school, raised five children, most of whom became professionals – all while never knowing how to read and write.

The experience was at once gratifying and frustrating. We had a nice rapport – at times it looked like we were making progress only to lead to frustration when it didn't stick for any length of time. This was not surprising. We had learned in training that people who never learned to read or write in any language when they were young were extremely resistant to learning in later life. Traumatic brain damage would also likely be a permanent obstacle. Still we kept the group together for almost a year. Attendance was erratic and library staff participation limited but I was motivated.

Then when Shirley became ill in the spring of 1999 Arnie and I started going to Tennessee every other week, often picking Benny up on the way, to visit her — first in the hospital and then a nursing home. It was both physically and emotionally draining. Ultimately I lost my drive to continue with the literacy program. When I broke the news to the group, despite that fact that they had made little progress, the idea that we were breaking up brought tears all around.

Seven years later, after we had moved to Syosset, Long Island I came across a small article in the newspaper that seemed to be written to me. It addressed the "catch 22" that people face in applying previous work experience to non-profit organizations; this because the non-profits look for years of not-for-profit work experience. To bridge that gap the Long Island Chapter of the Association of Fundraising Professionals was launching a three month internship program offering a small stipend for fifteen hours per week in participating organizations that might lead to part or full time permanent employment.

I immediately applied and went through the red tape to become perhaps the oldest intern ever. I was matched with the Long Island Chapter of the Juvenile Diabetes Research Association. The young women maintained their composure but couldn't hide their surprise upon seeing the new intern; with her deeply lined face, furrowed brow, sixty-seven year old hands; the term intern seemed like an oxymoron. It generally conjures a picture of a young, ambitious college student, not a well seasoned woman seeking a late-life personal reinvention.

At my age it turned out that there was plenty for me to learn and conversely to contribute. Finally I had the opportunity to use my experience. In the three months I worked at JDRF I put together a comprehensive "chapter brochure" as well as a public relations contact data base and I met some amazing kids who where living with Juvenile Diabetes with dignity and passion.

Unfortunately when the internship period ended there was no budget to keep me on payroll and their policy was to use volunteers only for temporary events; as for administration they hired full time personnel only.

A short time after I left, however, the executive director introduced me to a friend who was involved with another non-profit, a small local fish hatchery and environmental education center. I worked there part time as grant writer/administrator until last year when the worsening economy made it almost impossible to obtain grants.

Over the last ten years, I have taken the opportunity to devote more time to writing, a craft I have enjoyed since the age of seven when I was put to work as the family scribe – penning letters to big brother Benny away at college and family correspondence when Mom let it be known that she was ashamed of her foreign-looking handwriting.

I have written every day through my school years and career. Finally this passion has come full circle with this family memoir, a labor of love that has for me been a "work worth doing."

Chapter 70
Keeping Family Alive

At this writing, Mom and Dad have been gone for thirty-nine and forty-eight years respectively. Yet, I still hear their laughter, directives, and discussions. Often I hear them from my own lips as I find myself quoting one or both of them almost daily.

As mentioned early in this piece, on the concept of "life after death," Dad always made the argument that our lives continue on in those we leave behind:

"Sure there's life after death but unfortunately not for the deceased."

Add to this yet another Yogi-ism, *"you can observe a lot by watching"* and at this point in my life I have "watched" at least three generations, albeit the latter to a limited degree, and I have "observed" many indications that Dad was probably right.

It is clear that he and Mom continue to live. I see them through familiar behavior patterns of their children and grandchildren; through similar thought processes, idiosyncrasies, mannerisms and life choices — that are even evident in progeny with whom they had little or no contact.

There is no question Ben, while he resembled Mom, acted much like Dad. Dad also continues to live on in Ned, Ross and Neil in their nontraditional life choices; their desire and need to work for themselves regardless of monetary gain. Shirley carried Mom's hyper-worrying personality to new heights in raising Neil and Julie under her vigilant eye. Julie and Margo have inherited Shirley's creativity and craftsmanship — to name just a few traits that I have witnessed in what I regret has been much too little personal contact.

If the midwife Alice who helped usher me into this world were here today, she would likely prognosticate that Mama and Daddy will hang around for some time to come. Another new generation has already begun as of June 2009 with the birth of Noah's son Benjamin Beck — Mom and Dad's first great, great grandson and my great, great nephew. And, again to quote Yogi, perhaps the most quoted personality of our time:

"It ain't over till it's over,"

Brad's five offspring, already or quickly approaching parenting age, along with their cousins promise a veritable "Beck Baby Boom."

Seeds from the unions of Mom and Dad's parents' who married well over a century ago, are now woven, fully assimilated, into the American culture – from New York and Pennsylvania in the east – to Tennessee, Iowa, Ohio in the hrartland – to the Northwest corner in Washington state.

In line with the transitory nature of human existence, those who enjoy full and satisfying lives – even if they achieved fame, fortune or notoriety – are soon forgotten. Notwithstanding astounding technological advances that promise to significantly extend longevity, life's journey will likely remain akin to an adventurous vacation which, in retrospect, always seems to have zipped by in a flash.

As we make our way through a maze of highs and lows, joy and sorrow, achievement and disappointment, it feels like our lives will go on into infinity. From the rear-view mirror, however, we can't help but wonder where the years have gone.

I hope this will help preserve the memories of our ancestors just a little longer.

Author's Note

Remembering stories and events in the lives of my family and writing them down to the best of my recollection have helped me better understand my parents, siblings and myself. It has put many things in perspective and given me a sense of gratitude. I began to see that while we were poor, like many first-generation American families who suffered the indignities of poverty, we were also enriched by the history, wisdom, culture and strength of our ancestors.

They brought with them a heritage of endurance, independence and courage that lives on in their descendants.

They raised us to the best of their ability in a diverse environment where we experienced a wide variety of cultures; a cacophony of accents that permeated the streets, small friendly stores and stoops where people congregated, all of which have since faded away. Also lost were often untranslatable words, colloquial expressions and powerful proverbs that added color to our lives.

In the fifties, sixties and seventies, the generation of pioneering immigrants that added so much to this country died, leaving few remnants of their European roots – their inimitable, often unintentional omnipresent humor and wisdom gleaned through lives filled with spiritual richness, vibrancy and yes, death and destruction.

Their first-generation American offspring are likewise dying out, taking with them the last remaining vestiges of the rich cultures, vernacular and family memories made by their parents who worked hard to make lives of their children better. They encouraged us to take advantage of the opportunities this country offers to improve our lives – to educate ourselves, work hard, and most of all – to believe in ourselves. It is hard to imagine, given the hardships we endured, that we would ever feel the relative sense of satisfaction and security many of us enjoy today.

If, in these pages you have seen a little bit of yourself, your siblings or your children; if you feel somewhat more connected to your past; if any questions about *why* you are *who* you are have been answered; if you have learned from a look back at cultures that predated yours – and especially if you smiled here and there — perhaps you will be inspired to "pick up the torch" and continue to share your legacy as well as many good memories you are making today.

Whether you are related by blood, identify by generation, culture, or childhood experiences — or simply enjoy reading about earlier times — I urge you to try to write about your family legacy for future generations — both you and they will benefit from the effort.

Acknowledgements

Sincere thanks to my deceased Mom and Dad for providing strong, tenacious colorful main characters whom I dearly miss. Special thanks to my late brother and sister whom I grieve for as well, and whom I wish I could have consulted on many of these stories. My gratitude also to the other primary and secondary players portrayed here.

I acknowledge that I could not have completed this work without my husband, Arnie who generously listened to essay after essay – over and over again. I am grateful for his always candid, constructive criticism, patience and support to the end – to include his tireless proofreading and sound suggestions for the completed manuscript and cover.

I would also like to thank my daughter Robin Gortler for proofreading the manuscript to help make it as readable and comprehensible as possible.

I am equally grateful to my grandson Adam Gortler for his computer expertise, encouragement and help with the cover photos as well as his guidance through the navigation of the transmission process.

I am particularly appreciative of Taproot Writing Workshops and the Long Island Writers Guild for their indispensible educational and technical support. as well as the camaraderie I enjoyed with other writers throughout this process.

Heartfelt thanks to Maxwell C. Wheat, Taproot leader and inspirational educator extraordinaire and the many members of our Taproot group who have become good friends and motivated me with praise, positive suggestions and affection. I feel very lucky to have had the opportunity to meet new BFF's – Ursula Nouza, Marilyn Goldsmith and many others – at this time in my life.

I am also sincerely grateful to Peter Garanani, founder of the LIWG, for his inimitable insight, instruction and encouragement. My sincere appreciation to Dennis Kotch, President of this important non-profit organization and his wife, Beverly who kindly dedicate countless hours and know-how to helping each writer develop his or her voice and talent.

Thanks also to Jenny Legun, Senior Publishing Consultant and her team at CreateSpace.

Finally, I am indebted to my family, friends and readers. I hope you have enjoyed this labor of love, and that you experience close ties with your families of yesteryear, today and tomorrow.